GAA
QUIZ BOOK

GAA
QUIZ BOOK

Collins

Published in 2007 by HarperCollins Publishers

HarperCollins Publishers
77-85 Fulham Palace Road
London
W6 8JB

www.collins.co.uk

Reprint 10 9 8 7 6 5 4 3 2 1

ISBN 13 978-0-00-726356-1

A catalogue record for this book is available from the British Library.

Collins uses papers that are natural, renewable and recyclable products made from wood
grown in sustainable forests. The manufacturing processes conform to the environmental
regulations of the country of origin.

Typeset by seagulls.net

Printed and bound in Great Britain by Clays Ltd, St Ives plc.

Mixed Sources
Product group from well-managed
forests and other controlled sources
www.fsc.org Cert no. TT-COC-2139
© 1996 Forest Stewardship Council

THE QUIZZES

GENERAL KNOWLEDGE

1 Who holds the record for the most All-Ireland club football titles?

2 What was the nickname of the former Kerry forward Eoin Liston?

3 What club does DJ Carey play for?

4 Who won the 2006 Ulster football title?

5 Which rule was amended to allow soccer or rugby to be played on a tempoorary basis in Croke Park?

6 Who managed Tyrone to All-Ireland minor, U-21 and senior titles?

7 Who scored the winning goal for Offaly in the famous 1982 All-Ireland final against Kerry?

8 How many All-Ireland senior hurling medals did DJ Carey win?

9 Who captained the Cork hurlers to the Centenary Year (1984) All-Ireland title?

10 Where was that Centenary All-Ireland hurling final played?

11 Who captained Cork to the 2005 All-Ireland hurling title?

ANSWERS PAGE 199

12 Name the only player in history to win All-Ireland hurling and football medals in the same year.

13 Who won the 2007 Sigerson Cup title?

14 Who won the 2007 Fitzgibbon Cup title?

15 Name the former Dublin footballer who is chief executive of the Gaelic Players Association.

16 Who was appointed as the GAA Player Welfare manager in 2006 before taking up office at the outset of 2007?

17 Who captained Armagh to their first All-Ireland football title in 2002?

18 Name the former Kilkenny hurler and manager who was appointed GAA President in 2005.

19 Who captained Kerry to the Centenary Year All-Ireland football title?

20 Name the three players to captain their county to more than one All-Ireland senior hurling title over the last 25 years.

ANSWERS PAGE 199

FOOTBALL GENERAL KNOWLEDGE

21 What year did the All-Ireland football final between Kerry and Cavan take place at the Polo Grounds in New York?

22 Name the player who scored nine points out of Kerry's total of 0-13 in the 1997 All-Ireland final.

23 Who scored Kildare's only goal in their 1998 All-Ireland final defeat to Galway?

24 Who captained Cork in the 1999 All-Ireland Senior football final?

25 When did Down last win the All-Ireland football title?

26 How many games did Dublin and Meath play during their first round Leinster championship clash in 1991?

27 Who managed Clare to the 1992 Munster football title?

28 How many All-Ireland club titles have Crossmaglen Rangers won?

29 When did Roscommon last win a Connacht senior title?

30 What year did Fermanagh play in their first All-Ireland Senior football semi-final?

31 Who won the 2007 All-Ireland U-21 football title?

ANSWERS PAGE 199

32 Who was the first and only Wicklow footballer to be selected as an All-Star?

33 Name the only player of the modern era (the last 15 years) to be selected on the GAA's Football Team of the Millennium.

34 Larry Tompkins won All-Irelands with Cork in 1989 and 1990 but what county did Tompkins hail from?

35 This Dublin footballer won two All-Ireland medals and played 70 consecutive championship games before retiring in 1997. Name him.

36 What year was the qualifier system introduced in the All-Ireland football championship?

37 Name the Tyrone footballer who scored 11 points from play in the 1984 Ulster final against Armagh.

38 Name the former Armagh footballer who managed St Galls to the 2005 Ulster club football title.

39 Which player won Footballer of the Year in 2006?

40 Which player won Young Footballer of the Year in 2006?

ANSWERS PAGE 199

MANAGERIAL ROLL CALL 1

41 How many counties has Mick O'Dwyer managed?

42 How many senior All-Irelands did Cyril Farrell win as manager of Galway?

43 How many senior All-Irelands did Kevin Heffernan win as manager of Dublin?

44 Who coached Offaly to their first All-Ireland hurling title in 1981?

45 Who managed Derry to their first All-Ireland in 1993?

46 How many Munster titles did Ger Loughnane win as manager of Clare?

47 How many All-Irelands did Sean Boylan win as manager of Meath?

48 How many Ulster titles did Joe Kernan win as manager of Armagh?

49 Who managed Kilkenny to successive All-Irelands in 1982 and '83?

50 How many Connacht titles did John O'Mahony win as manager of Galway?

51 Who managed Donegal to their first All-Ireland title in 1992?

ANSWERS PAGE 199

52 Who managed Offaly to the 1982 All-Ireland football title?

53 After he stepped down as Tipperary manager in 1994, who did Michael 'Babs' Keating subsequently manage between 1996 and 1997?

54 Who managed Down to their two All-Irelands in 1991 and 1994?

55 Who managed Kilkenny to successive All-Irelands in 1992 and 1993?

56 How many counties has Paidi O Se managed?

57 Who was the coach to Cork's three-in a row All-Ireland hurling winning team of 1976-78?

58 Who coached Offaly to successive All-Ireland football titles in 1971 and 1972?

59 How many Munster football titles did Billy Morgan win with Cork during his first managerial term between 1987 and 1996?

60 Name the only player ever to captain and manage a side to All-Ireland glory in the same season.

ANSWERS PAGE 199

HURLING GENERAL KNOWLEDGE

61 Name the Tipperary hurler who scored 2-1 in the 2001 All-Ireland hurling final against Galway.

62 Name the first club to win consecutive All-Ireland hurling titles.

63 Who captained Galway in the 2005 All-Ireland final?

64 What year did Offaly win their last All-Ireland title?

65 Prior to 2007, what year did Limerick's senior hurlers last win the All-Ireland title?

66 Who captained Antrim to the 2007 Ulster hurling title?

67 Who managed Offaly to the 2000 All-Ireland final?

68 Name the only hurler from the modern era to be selected on the GAA's official Team of the Millennium.

69 What year did DJ Carey sensationally first announce his retirement from hurling?

70 What year did DJ Carey captain Kilkenny to an All-Ireland senior hurling title?

71 Who did the Antrim hurlers defeat in the 1989 All-Ireland senior hurling semi-final?

72 Name the Antrim manager that year.

ANSWERS PAGE 199

73 Name the manager who led Cork to the 2005 All-Ireland hurling title.

74 Who captained Tipperary to the 1989 All-Ireland title?

75 Prior to 2007, how many senior hurling titles had Limerick won?

76 What did Dan Shanahan score in the 2007 Munster final?

77 Who captained Cork to the 2000 Munster title?

78 When did Offaly and Kilkenny last contest a Leinster final?

79 How many times did Christy Ring captain Cork to All-Ireland hurling titles?

80 How many All-Ireland finals between 1996 and 2006 failed to produce a goal?

DUAL PLAYERS

81 Name the Cork player who played in All-Ireland hurling and football finals in 1999.

82 As well as being a prominent Laois footballer, this player also won a Division Two National Hurling League medal in 2007. Who is he?

83 How many All-Ireland senior medals did Jimmy Barry-Murphy win in both codes?

84 Name the player who played in All-Ireland hurling and football finals in 1981.

85 What year did Brian Corcoran play in an All-Ireland senior football final

86 Tommy Carew was a great dual player with which county?

87 Name the Down player who won All-Ireland football titles in 1991 and 1994 but who also won an Ulster hurling title in 1992?

88 Name the Galway hurler who played in the 2001 All-Ireland hurling final and who also played in the 2000 Connacht football championship against Sligo?

89 Michael 'Babs' Keating won a Railway Cup football medal with Munster in which year?

90 Name the Derry player who was nominated for an All-Star award in both hurling and football in 2000.

ANSWERS PAGE 200

91 Who is the only player to win All-Ireland senior medals in six successive years?

92 Name the current Mayo footballer who won a Railway Cup hurling medal with Connacht in 2004.

93 Name the Tipperary player who played in Munster hurling and football finals in 2002.

94 Name the Limerick player who played in Munster football finals in 2003 and 2004 and who played in the 2007 Munster hurling final?

95 Name the Cork player who won Munster medals in hurling and football in 1990.

96 Name the player who captained Cork in the 1967 All-Ireland football final and who was named Hurler of the Year in 1977.

97 Name the only Galway player to win All-Ireland senior medals in both hurling and football.

98 Name the Wexford player who won five All-Ireland medals (one hurling and four football) between 1910 and 1918.

99 What year did Dinny Allen win a Munster senior hurling title with Cork?

100 Who was the first player chosen as both a hurling and football All-Star in the same year?

ANSWERS PAGE 200

ALL-IRELAND SENIOR HURLING FINALS

101 Who captained Kilkenny to the 2000 All-Ireland title?

102 How many counties won the Liam MacCarthy Cup in the 1990s?

103 Who were Offaly's two goalscorers in the 1998 All-Ireland final win?

104 Who were Galway's two goalscorers in the 2001 All-Ireland final?

105 Kilkenny scored five goals in the 2000 final but when was the last time a county scored five goals in an All-Ireland final before 2000?

106 How many All-Ireland finals did Galway contest in the 1980s?

107 This player captained Cork to the 1986 All-Ireland title before he became manager of Cork for one season in 2001. Who is he?

108 Which Wexford forward was the top scorer in the 1996 All-Ireland final?

109 Who came on as a substitute to score Clare's only goal in the 1995 All-Ireland final?

110 When did Dublin last win an All-Ireland senior title?

ANSWERS PAGE 200

111 Which year did Cork score five goals in an All-Ireland final and still lose?

112 Where was the first All-Ireland hurling final played in 1888?

113 In what year did it take three games to decide the All-Ireland hurling final?

114 Excluding the 1984 Centenary All-Ireland final, where and when was the last time an All-Ireland hurling final was played outside Croke Park?

115 Who captained Tipperary in the 1997 All-Ireland final?

116 True or False. Prior to 2007, Glasgow had a better record in All-Ireland quarter-finals than Limerick.

117 In the last ten years, two brothers captained their county in All-Ireland finals. Name them.

118 What was unique about the 0-13 to 0-12 scoreline in the 1999 All-Ireland final between Cork and Kilkenny?

119 Name the Wexford goalkeeper who made a late and famous save in the 1956 All-Ireland final from Christy Ring.

120 Who were the only father and son to captain teams in senior hurling finals?

ANSWERS PAGE 200

FOOTBALL GENERAL KNOWLEDGE

121 Name the Meath footballer who came on as a substitute in the 1997 replayed Leinster semi-final against Kildare and changed the match by scoring four points?

122 Who won Tipperary's first ever football All-Star?

123 Who was Laois' sole representative on the GAA's official football Team of the Millennium

124 Who captained Tyrone to their first ever All-Ireland football title in 2003

125 How many points did Galway footballer Padraig Joyce score in the 2001 All-Ireland final?

126 Who captained Tyrone to the 2005 All-Ireland senior football title?

127 Name the goalkeeper on the Armagh All-Ireland winning team of 2002.

128 Who captained Galway to the 2001 All-Ireland Senior title?

129 Who captained Dublin to the 2003 All-Ireland U-21 football title?

130 Who captained Galway to the 1998 All-Ireland football title?

131 Who captained Meath to the 1996 All-Ireland title?

ANSWERS PAGE 200

132 Which county won four Connacht titles in a row between 1977 and 1980?

133 What was the scoreline in the 1982 All-Ireland final between Offaly and Kerry?

134 Which two players lifted the trophy after Galway won the 2005 Connacht championship?

135 When did Louth last win an All-Ireland senior football title?

136 How many All-Ireland club titles did Joe Kernan win as manager of Crossmaglen Rangers

137 Who managed Ballinderry to the 2002 All-Ireland club title?

138 Which player scored the only two goals of the game in the 2007 Connacht football quarter-final between Galway and Mayo?

139 In 2001, Derry and Galway reached an All-Ireland semi-final through the back door but they defeated two sides in the All-Ireland quarter-finals that had already beaten them in their provincial championships. Name those two sides.

140 What was the first ever game played in the All-Ireland football qualifiers?

ANSWERS PAGE 200

FAMINE ENDINGS

141 What year did Offaly win their first All-Ireland hurling title?

142 When Galway won the 1998 All-Ireland football title, they ended an All-Ireland famine which had stretched for how many years?

143 Which county finally won a senior football championship match in 2000 after 18 years?

144 Which county ended a 57-year famine in 1980 to win an All-Ireland title?

145 Clare won the 1995 All-Ireland hurling title but when had they won their previous All-Ireland?

146 Which county ended a 57-year famine to win a provincial senior title in 2003?

147 Which county won their first provincial senior title in 2004?

148 When Clare won the 1992 Munster senior final, how many years had it been since their previous provincial title?

149 When Wexford won the 1996 All-Ireland hurling title, how many years had it been since their previous All-Ireland title?

150 When Limerick won the 1994 Munster hurling title, it was their first provincial title since what year

151 Which Ulster county won a Senior championship game in 1999 for the first time in eight years?

152 Which county ended a 92-year famine for a provincial title in 2000?

153 When Offaly won the 1997 Leinster title, it was their first provincial football title since what year?

154 When Kildare won the 1998 Leinster football title, it was their first provincial title since what year?

155 Which county ended a 29-year famine to win a provincial title in 1997?

156 Which county ended a 52-year wait for a provincial hurling title in 1992?

157 When Waterford won the 2002 Munster hurling title, it had been how many years since their previous title?

158 What county won their first All-Ireland senior football title in 1971?

159 When Waterford defeated Clare in the 2007 Munster football championship, they finally won a championship game after how many years?

160 Name the Tipperary captain who famously declared 'The famine is over' after Tipperary won the 1987 Munster title after 16 years.

ALL-IRELAND FINAL BAND OF BROTHERS

161 Name the two brothers who captained their county to All-Ireland finals in football and hurling in successive years in the 1990s.

162 How many All-Irelands did Joe, Johnny and Billy Dooley win together (on the same team) with Offaly?

163 Name the two brothers that captained their county to All-Ireland hurling success in the last 15 years.

164 How many All-Ireland medals did Andy and Martin Comerford win together with Kilkenny?

165 Galway had two sets of brothers on the team that won the 2001 All-Ireland final against Meath. Name them.

166 Name the two sets of brothers who played in the 1997 All-Ireland hurling final between Clare and Tipperary.

167 Name the three sets of twins to have won All-Ireland hurling and football medals in the last 15 years.

168 Name the three sets of brothers who played for Offaly in the 1998 All-Ireland hurling final.

169 Name the two sets of brothers who played for Armagh in the 2002 All-Ireland football final.

170 Name the two brothers Donegal had in their starting forward line for the 1992 All-Ireland football final.

ANSWERS PAGE 200

171 Two sets of brothers started for Tyrone in the 1995 All-Ireland final. Name them.

172 Between the drawn and replayed All-Ireland football final in 2000, Galway used four sets of brothers. Name them.

173 Name the only two sets of three brothers to win All-Ireland football medals on the field of play between 1986 and 2006.

174 Name the two sets of brothers who played for Limerick in the 1996 All-Ireland hurling final.

175 Two brothers have been goalkeepers for the same county in All-Ireland football finals over the last 15 years. Name them.

176 Name the two sets of brothers who played in the 2001 All-Ireland hurling final between Tipperary and Galway.

177 Apart from Joe, Johnny and Billy Dooley, name the only other three brothers who played in an All-Ireland hurling final together over the last 15 years.

178 Name the two sets of brothers that played for Cork in the 2006 All-Ireland hurling final.

179 Three sets of brothers played in the 1993 All-Ireland football final between Derry and Cork. Name them.

180 At the end of the 1982 All-Ireland football final, how many sets of brothers did Offaly have on the field?

ANSWERS PAGE 200

GENERAL KNOWLEDGE

181 Name the famed Kilkenny hurling school which has won the most All-Ireland colleges titles.

182 What county won three All-Ireland U-21 hurling titles in a row between 2000 and 2002?

183 Who captained Tyrone to the 1998 All-Ireland minor title?

184 What club does Tipperary's Lar Corbett play for?

185 Who became the first President of the GAA?

186 Who managed the Tipperary hurlers to All-Ireland titles in 1989 and 1991?

187 When Tipperary won the 1989 All-Ireland title, how many years had it been since their previous All-Ireland success?

188 Who captained Meath to the 1999 All-Ireland football title?

189 Tony Browne captained the Waterford U-21 hurlers to their first All-Ireland U-21 title in what year?

190 What year did Brian Whelehan play in his first senior All-Ireland semi-final for Offaly?

191 When Liam Hassett captained the Kerry footballers to the 1997 All-Ireland title, who did he take over the captaincy from after that year's Munster final?

192 Name the Kerry captain who delivered his All-Ireland winning speech in 2004 in Irish.

193 Name the former Laois player who managed Wexford to the 2005 National Football League final.

194 When former Armagh footballer Ger Houlahan chose to play in the first round of the 1994 Ulster championship against Fermanagh, what big event did he miss out on the same day?

195 Which province has won the least number of Interprovincial football championships (formerly Railway Cup)?

196 Which county won the first ever Tommy Murphy Cup title in 2004?

197 Which county won the inaugural Christy Ring Cup title in 2005?

198 Which team won the first ever Nicky Rackard Cup title in 2005?

199 Which county played in five successive National Hurling League finals between 1952 and 1957?

200 Which Tipperary hurler won the first Texaco Hurler of the Year award in 1958?

ANSWERS PAGE 201

TRUE OR FALSE

201 Offaly were the first county to reach an All-Ireland hurling final through the back door.

202 Former Kildare footballer Brian Lacey played minor hurling for Tipperary.

203 Antrim lost the 1979 Leinster minor hurling final to Kilkenny.

204 The Clare minor hurlers were the first inter-county team to win an All-Ireland hurling title through the back door.

205 John Gardiner plays his club hurling with Blackrock.

206 Prior to 2007 Clare had played in 11 Munster U-21 hurling finals but had only won one.

207 Eugene Cloonan was the goalkeeper on the Galway U-21 hurling team that won the 1996 All-Ireland title.

208 Wicklow club Rathnew won nine county senior football titles in a row between the mid-1990s and 2005.

209 A Tipperary club and a Kilkenny club have met only once in the All-Ireland club hurling championship.

210 The legendary Nickey Rackard from Wexford was on the GAA's official Hurling Team of the Millennium.

211 Waterford won the 2000 Munster U-21 football title.

212 Jamesie O'Connor played minor football for Clare before he played minor hurling.

213 On Mick O'Dwyer's senior championship debut as a player, Kerry were beaten by Waterford.

214 Offaly reached three All-Ireland U-21 hurling finals between 1989 and 1992 but only won one title.

215 Dan Shanahan scored three goals against Clare in the 2004 Munster hurling quarter-final.

216 Brian Cody captained Kilkenny to the 1983 All-Ireland hurling title.

217 Crossmolina Deel Rovers have won two All-Ireland club football titles.

218 Galway won three Connacht football titles in a row between 2000-2002.

219 The great Kerry goalkeeper Dan O'Keeffe was born in Co Cork.

220 The Brazilian soccer legend Socrates won a Sigerson Cup medal with UCD.

ANSWERS PAGE 201

NAME THE YEAR 1

221 Joe Connolly captains Galway to an All-Ireland hurling title.

222 Birr become the first club to win four All-Ireland club hurling titles.

223 Tommy Lyons manages Dublin to a Leinster football title.

224 Kilkenny win their first National Hurling league title under Brian Cody.

225 Hubert Rigney captains Offaly to an All-Ireland hurling title.

226 Dara O Cinneide plays wing-back for Kerry in a Munster football final against Cork.

227 Mickey Moran manages Sligo to a Connacht final.

228 Ballygunner win their first Munster club hurling title.

229 Rathnew win their first Leinster club football title.

230 Nicky English manages Tipperary to a Munster hurling final against Waterford.

231 Carlow defeat Down in the semi-final to reach their first Christy Ring Cup final.

232 Alan Browne captains Cork to a Munster hurling title.

ANSWERS PAGE 201

233 Eoin Kelly captains LIT to their first Fitzgibbon Cup title, scoring 1–9 in the final.

234 Tommy Dunne scores two goals in a Munster hurling final for Tipperary against Cork.

235 Peter Canavan wins his first Ulster senior title with Tyrone.

236 Johnny Dooley scores 0–12 for Offaly in an All-Ireland quarter-final against Derry.

237 Waterford win their first Munster U-21 football title.

238 Donegal contest their first Nicky Rackard Cup final.

239 Len Gaynor manages Clare to a Munster hurling final against Tipperary.

240 Teddy McCarthy wins the Texaco Footballer of the Year award.

GENERAL KNOWLEDGE

241 What year did Donegal win their first ever All-Ireland senior football title?

242 Which college boasts the most Sigerson Cup titles?

243 What club did Eddie Keher play for?

244 Where is the All-Ireland Poc Fada Competition annually held?

245 Which former Limerick hurler guided Offaly to the 1994 All-Ireland senior hurling title, beating Limerick in the final?

246 Who was the top scorer in the 2005 All-Ireland senior football final with 0-5?

247 Who led Offaly to the 1998 All-Ireland senior hurling title after Michael 'Babs' Keating controversially stepped down after that year's Leinster final defeat to Kilkenny?

248 Who managed the Laois senior hurlers in 2007?

249 What year did Guinness take over the sponsorship of the senior hurling championship?

250 Which county has the most GAA clubs in Ireland?

251 Name the manager who led Mayo to the 2001 National League title.

ANSWERS PAGE 202

252 Who was the top scorer in the 2005 All-Ireland senior football championship?

253 How many games did Tyrone play to win the 2005 All-Ireland title?

254 Who was the top scorer in the 2005 All-Ireland senior hurling championship?

255 Who managed Kildare to the 2003 Leinster football final?

256 Who captained Leitrim to their last Connacht senior title in 1994?

257 What year did Kevin Fennelly manage Kilkenny to a Leinster senior hurling title?

258 Name the only two counties never to have won provincial senior football titles.

259 Who was the top scorer in the 2003 All-Ireland football final with 0-5?

260 How many years was Sean Boylan manager of Meath?

REFEREES

Name the county of the following referees

261 Dickie Murphy

262 Brian Crowe

263 Seamus Roche

264 John Bannon

265 Brian White

266 Diarmuid Kirwan

267 John Geaney

268 Eamonn Morris

269 Barry Kelly

270 Pat McEnaney

271 Aidan Mangan

272 Michael Wadding

273 Sean McMahon

274 Marty Duffy

275 Pat O'Connor

276 Michael Collins

277 Paddy Russell

278 Michael Haverty

279 Vincent Neary

280 Brian Gavin

ANSWERS PAGE 202

TEXACO HURLER AND FOOTBALLER OF THE YEAR OVER THE LAST 15 YEARS

HURLING

281 Larry O'Gorman won the award in what season?

282 Who won the award in 1997?

283 Which two years did Brian Corcoran win the award?

284 Which Clare player won it in 1995?

285 Henry Shefflin won his first Texaco hurler of the year in what season?

286 Brian Whelehan won his two awards in which seasons?

287 Which Kilkenny player scooped the award in 2003?

288 Name the Cork player selected in 2004.

289 Name the Cork player selected in 2005.

290 Which Tipperary player won the award in 2001?

ANSWERS PAGE 202

FOOTBALL

291 Down's Mickey Linden won the award in which season?

292 Name the Dublin player selected in 1995.

293 Who won the award in 2003?

294 Which Donegal player was selected in 1992?

295 Who won the award in 1997?

296 Trevor Giles was selected in what year?

297 Who won the award in 2004?

298 Which Galway player took the prize in 1998?

299 Which Galway player took the prize in 2001?

300 Who won the award in 2000

CLUB HURLERS

Name the club of the following hurlers

301 Eamonn Corcoran (Tipperary)

302 Henry Shefflin (Kilkenny)

303 Tom Kenny (Cork)

304 Seamus Prendergast (Waterford)

305 Declan Ruth (Wexford)

306 Brendan Murphy (Offaly)

307 Gerry Quinn (Clare)

308 David Collins (Galway)

309 Dan Shanahan (Waterford)

310 Kevin Flynn (Dublin)

311 John Tennyson (Kilkenny)

312 Ollie Moran (Limerick)

313 James Young (Laois)

314 Timmy McCarthy (Cork)

315 Liam Watson (Antrim)

316 Brian O'Connell (Clare)

317 Derek Lyng (Kilkenny)

318 Eoin Kelly (Waterford)

319 Rory McCarthy (Wexford)

320 Kevin Broderick (Galway)

ANSWERS PAGE 202

GENERAL KNOWLEDGE

321 Who captained Mayo in the 2006 All-Ireland football final?

322 Who captained Cork in the 2006 All-Ireland hurling final?

323 Which Tyrone player scored a penalty against Armagh in the 2005 All-Ireland semi-final?

324 Name the referee who refereed a Connacht club hurling semi-final in 2006 and who subsequently played in the 2007 All-Ireland club final.

325 Which college won the Fitzgibbon Cup title for the first time in 2005?

326 Which Offaly hurler scored 1-6 in the 1998 All-Ireland final against Kilkenny?

327 Which Waterford hurler from Ballygunner won his first All-Star in 2004?

328 Who managed Down to the 2003 Ulster football final?

329 Who scored Kilkenny's two goals in the 2007 Leinster hurling final?

330 Name the father and son who made their senior inter-county hurling debuts as a manager and player in the Liam MacCarthy Cup in 2007.

ANSWERS PAGE 202

331 Which Kilkenny club did Athenry defeat in the 2001 All-Ireland club final after extra-time?

332 What club does Tyrone's Brian McGuigan play for?

333 Name the hotel in Thurles where the foundation meeting of the GAA was held in 1884.

334 Which former All-Ireland winner and well-known current radio broadcaster wrote the book on the legendary Dr Eamonn O'Sullivan *Man Before His Time*?

335 Name the legendary Tipperary player who was selected on the GAA's Hurling Team of the Millennium and who played in a record four All-Ireland minor finals, winning three titles.

336 Who captained Portumna to the 2006 All-Ireland club hurling title?

337 What year did Waterford win their first All-Ireland senior hurling title?

338 Which legendary Dublin football player and manager was inducted into the GAA's Hall of Fame in 1998?

339 How many All-Ireland senior football titles have Louth won?

340 Who captained Kilkenny in the 1999 All-Ireland hurling final?

GENERAL KNOWLEDGE

341 In which town is the Gaelic games interpretative centre called 'Lár na Páirce'?

342 After which former Kilkenny hurler is the GAA Heritage Centre in Tullaroan named?

343 What is the regulation height (in metres) for a GAA crossbar from the ground?

344 How many provincial councils are there in the GAA?

345 Which month is the GAA Congress held?

346 Which company sponsored the All-Stars when they were selected by ballot of inter-county players, in the mid-1990s?

347 Prior to 2007, how many All-Ireland Senior Softball Singles handball titles did Michael 'Ducksie' Walsh win?

348 What is the name given to the inter-provincial championships in camogie?

349 From which county is the All-Ireland champion handballer Eoin Kennedy?

350 How many goals did Dan Shanahan score in the drawn and replayed All-Ireland quarter-finals against Cork in 2007?

351 What is the name of the trophy for the premier division of the All-Ireland Féile na nGael?

ANSWERS PAGE 203

352 Who is the current Patron of the GAA?

353 In which city is the GAA club called Aidan McAnespie's?

354 Which club has won the most county senior championship titles in a single code, football or hurling?

355 Which player was sent off in the All-Ireland Senior Football final of 1995 but did not leave the pitch until several minutes later?

356 Tánaiste and Minister for Finance Brian Cowen played under-21 football for which county?

357 Where was the first meeting of the Gaelic Players' Association held, in 1999?

358 The GAA's Annual Congress was only once held outside of Ireland, in 1996. Where was the venue?

359 Two former All-Ireland football winning captains stood unsuccessfully in the 2007 general elections. Name them.

360 Between 1990 and 2007, how many clubs called 'Rangers' have won the All-Ireland Club SFC title?

ALL-IRELAND FOOTBALL SEMI-FINALS

361 Who did Tyrone beat in the 2003 semi-final?

362 Who hit the post with a late free for Dublin against Armagh in the 2002 semi-final?

363 How many semi-finals in a row did Kerry contest between 2000 and 2006 (inclusive)?

364 Who did Mayo defeat in the 1997 semi-final?

365 How many semi-finals has John Maughan managed teams (excluding replays) to?

366 Who were Armagh's two goalscorers in their 2003 semi-final win?

367 Who did Galway defeat in the 2000 semi-final?

368 How many semi-finals did Armagh contest between 1999 and 2006?

369 Which county did Donegal beat in the 1992 semi-final?

370 Who did Dublin defeat in the 1995 semi-final?

371 When was the last time a semi-final was played outside Croke Park?

372 Who managed Derry in the 2004 semi-final?

ANSWERS PAGE 203

373 Who scored the winning point for Derry against Dublin in the 1993 semi-final?

374 Who managed Cork to the 2002 semi-final?

375 Which Kerry player scored a penalty against Armagh in the 2000 drawn semi-final?

376 What year did two Munster teams first contest a semi-final against one another?

377 What year did two Ulster teams first contest a semi-final against each other?

378 What year did two teams from the 'back door' first contest a semi-final against each other?

379 Prior to 2007, who were the last county to score five goals in a semi-final (it happened in the last 15 years)?

380 Which were the only football county to win six successive semi-finals?

PAST COUNTY HURLERS
Name their clubs

381 John Fenton (Cork)

382 Fergal Hartley (Waterford)

383 Noel Skehan (Kilkenny)

384 Nicky English (Tipperary)

385 Conor Hayes (Galway)

386 Liam Dunne (Wexford)

387 Ger Cunningham (Cork)

388 Anthony Daly (Clare)

389 Stephen McDonagh (Limerick)

390 Brian Cody (Kilkenny)

391 Johnny Dooley (Offaly)

392 Gerry McInerney (Galway)

393 Terence McNaughton (Antrim)

394 John Leahy (Tipperary)

395 Ciaran Carey (Limerick)

396 Ger Henderson (Kilkenny)

397 Niall Rigney (Laois)

398 Eamonn Morrissey (Kilkenny and Dublin)

399 Noel Sands (Down)

400 Liam Doyle (Clare)

ANSWERS PAGE 203

ALL-IRELAND MINOR HURLING AND FOOTBALL CAPTAINS OVER THE LAST 15 YEARS

401 Andrew Keary captained which All-Ireland minor winning side in 2005?

402 David Flynn captained which All-Ireland minor winning team in 2006?

403 Greg Kennedy captained the Galway hurlers to an All-Ireland title in which year?

404 James Colgan captained which All-Ireland winning football team in 2005?

405 John Culkin captained which All-Ireland winning hurling team in 1999?

406 Conor O'Donovan captained the Galway minors to All-Ireland success in what year?

407 Brian O'Keeffe captained the Cork minors to which year's All-Ireland title?

408 What year did John Lee captain Galway to an All-Ireland minor hurling title?

409 James Masters captained Cork to All-Ireland minor football success in what season?

ANSWERS PAGE 203

410 Michael Rice captained Kilkenny to hurling success in which year?

411 Which Kilkenny player, who won an All-Ireland senior title in 2006, captained Kilkenny to an All-Ireland title in 2003?

412 Richie Murray captained Galway to an All-Ireland hurling title in which season?

413 Peter Donnelly captained Tyrone minors to an All-Ireland in which season?

414 Ger O'Kane captained which county to an All-Ireland football success in 2002?

415 Which county did Craig Rogers captain to All-Ireland minor success in the last five years?

416 Kieran Kelly captained which team to All-Ireland minor success in the last decade?

417 Who captained Westmeath to a historic All-Ireland football title in 1995?

418 Willie Maher captained which county to All-Ireland minor hurling success in the last 15 years?

419 Who captained Clare to the 1997 All-Ireland minor hurling title?

420 Philly Larkin was the Kilkenny minor captain in 1991 but he was suspended for the All-Ireland final. Who captained the victorious Kilkenny team in his place?

ANSWERS PAGE 203

GENERAL KNOWLEDGE

421 What club did the legendary Mick Mackey play for in Limerick?

422 How many Presidential terms of office did Maurice Davin serve?

423 What band founded by the Irish Christian Brothers first performed for the GAA in 1886?

424 Who captained Galway to the 2005 All-Ireland U-21 hurling title?

425 Which two years did DJ Carey win the Texaco Hurler of the Year Award?

426 Who captained Mayo to the 2006 All-Ireland U-21 football title?

427 Christy Heffernan won an All-Ireland club medal in 1991 with which Kilkenny club?

428 Name the Laois club that Birr defeated in Leinster club hurling finals in 1997, 1999 and 2001.

429 What year did O'Donovan Rossa (Cork) win the All-Ireland club football title?

430 Name the Dublin forward who kicked eight points in the replayed Leinster football quarter-final against Meath in 2007.

ANSWERS PAGE 204

431 Name the Cork goalkeeper who played in the 2007 Munster hurling semi-final against Waterford.

432 Which former Dublin player managed the Derry senior footballers in the late 1990s?

433 Which club did current Dublin football manager Paul Caffrey manage to an All-Ireland club final in 2000?

434 How many All-Ireland club football finals did Eire Og (Carlow) contest?

435 What year did Laois win their only All-Ireland senior hurling title?

436 Who was the first Clare player to receive a hurling All-Star?

437 Name the three brothers that scored 3-7 from play between them in the 2007 All-Ireland club hurling final.

438 Name the two Galway players who scored 6-3 between them in the 2005 All-Ireland U-21 football final.

439 Who was the only player to win two Railway Cup medals on the same day?

440 Name the only other player to win Railway Cup medals in the same year.

FIRSTS

441 What year did Donegal win their first National League football title?

442 What year did DJ Carey win his first All-Ireland senior hurling medal with Kilkenny?

443 What county became the first from the six counties to win the All-Ireland senior football title?

444 Who were the first hurling club to win back-to-back All-Ireland club titles?

445 What year did Tyrone reach their first ever All-Ireland senior football final?

446 Who were the first football club to win back-to-back All-Ireland club titles

447 What year did the Combined Universities win their first and only Interprovincial Football title (formerly Railway Cup)?

448 What year did Nemo Rangers win their first All-Ireland club football title?

449 What year did Offaly win their first Leinster senior hurling title?

450 What year did Waterford RTC (Now Waterford IT) win their first Fitzgibbon Cup title?

451 What year did IT Sligo win their first Sigerson Cup title?

452 What year did Peter Quinn take office as the first Fermanagh man to be elected President of the GAA?

453 Who was the first Waterford footballer to win an Interprovincial (Railway Cup) medal?

454 Gus Ryan captained what county to their first All-Ireland U-21 hurling title in 1987?

455 Who became the first and only player from Down to win All-Ireland minor, U-21 and senior football medals (on the field of play)?

456 Which counties met in the first ever football game played under floodlights at Croke Park?

457 What year did Henry Shefflin win his first All-Star award?

458 What year did Ballyhale Shamrocks win their first All-Ireland club hurling title?

459 Who was the first man from the six counties to lift the Sam Maguire Cup as Captain?

460 Who was the first man to win All-Ireland senior medals in hurling and football?

MUNSTER SENIOR HURLING FINALS

461 Who captained Waterford to the 2004 Munster title?

462 How many Munster hurling finals did Clare play in during the 1990s?

463 How many Munster hurling titles did Clare win during the 1990s?

464 How many Munster hurling finals did Waterford contest between 1998 and 2007 inclusive (excluding replays)?

465 How many Munster titles did Cork win between 1982 and 1986 inclusive?

466 Before 1998, when was the last time a Munster final had ended in a draw?

467 Name the Limerick forward who scored 1-3 in the 2001 Munster final.

468 Who captained Tipperary to the 1988 Munster title?

469 What year did Waterford win their first Munster hurling title?

470 What year was the first 80-minute Munster final played?

471 Who scored 3-1 in the 2003 Munster final and still ended up on the losing side?

ANSWERS PAGE 204

472 When was the last time a Munster final was held in the Gaelic Grounds in Limerick?

473 Name the Limerick player who scored 0-10 in the 1996 drawn Munster final.

474 Who captained Tipperary in the 2006 Munster final?

475 When did Tipperary last win three Munster titles in a row?

476 Who captained Cork to the 1990 Munster title?

477 Name the Limerick forward who scored 3-3 in the 1981 Munster final.

478 Name the Cork forward who scored 4-0 in the 1982 Munster final?

479 Name the Cork forward who scored 0-12 in the same game.

480 Name the Limerick player who lined out in the 1996 Munster final replay and subsequently played for UCC in the Cork county championship later that evening.

CLUBCALL 1

Name the county of the following clubs

481 Four Masters

482 O'Callaghan's Mills

483 Cargin

484 Newtown Blues

485 Glynn-Barntown

486 Cooley Kickhams

487 Dromintee

488 Kilrossanty

489 Naomh Eoin, Myshall

490 Carrickshock

491 Bunninadden

492 Scoil Ui Chonaill

493 The Heath

494 Clonguish

495 Walsh Island

496 The Downs

497 Arravale Rovers

498 Gowna

499 Garryspillane

500 Kilmoyley

ANSWERS PAGE 204

GAA PLAYERS WHO PLAYED OTHER CODES

501 Name the Dublin footballer who transferred sports to play with Manchester United in the 1970s.

502 Name the Cork footballer who played in a National League final and an FAI Cup final in successive weeks in 1989.

503 Niall Quinn played in an All-Ireland minor hurling final for Dublin in what year?

504 The current Irish soccer international Shane Long played minor hurling with which county?

505 Mick Galwey played championship football for which county?

506 The current Meath goalkeeper, Brendan Murphy, was a member of which club in the Premiership during the 1990s?

507 Celtic's Neil Lennon played in an Ulster minor football final in 1989 with what county?

508 Current Cork hurler Cathal Naughton was a member of which English soccer club for two seasons?

509 Name the Derry All-Ireland medal winner from 1993 who played a reserve game for Manchester United.

510 Name the Meath All-Ireland winner from 1996 and 1999 who had a trial at Arsenal.

511 Seamie Crowe, who played alongside Robbie Keane at Wolverhampton Wanderers, won an All-Ireland club football medal with which club?

512 Name the former Mayo midfielder who played in the 1996 All-Ireland final and who also played international basketball for Ireland.

513 Former Irish rugby international Eric Elwood played championship football for which county in 1989?

514 Keith Wood played U-16 hurling with which county in 1988?

515 Former Dublin footballer Dessie Farrel played hurling and what other sport at a high level?

516 Name the Galway footballer who caused a stir when signing for Galway United in 2001.

517 Name the former Galway midfielder who played in the 1998 and 2001 All-Ireland finals and also played international underage basketball.

518 Name the current Donegal footballer who has extensively played soccer in the Irish League.

519 Former Irish rugby international Moss Keane won three Sigerson Cup medals with which college?

520 Tom Furlong was a former inter-county footballer who later went on to become a place kicker in American football with the New York Giants and the Atlanta Falcons. Which county was Furlong from?

ANSWERS PAGE 204

FOOTBALL GENERAL KNOWLEDGE

521 Who was the first Leitrim footballer to win an All-Star award in 1990?

522 The GAA grounds in Enniskillen are named after a former Fermanagh player, whose two sons have been prominent county footballers over the last number of years. Who is that player?

523 Who were Galway's two representatives on the GAA Football Team of the Millennium?

524 Name the sportsman who was engaged in two major events on the same day in April 2007 – one in Limerick and the other in Croke Park.

525 Name the current Meath footballer who is a son of a former All-Ireland winning player from 1987 and 1988.

526 The record attendance at a GAA game was 90,556. Name the year and the occasion.

527 True or false. Fergal Byron played corner-back on the Laois U-21 team that won the 1994 Leinster title.

528 The bookmaker and boxing trainer Barney Eastwood won an All-Ireland minor football title with which county in 1948?

529 Who managed Westmeath to their Leinster senior title in 2004?

ANSWERS PAGE 205

530 How many All-Ireland minor finals did current Laois senior player Brian 'Beano' McDonald play in?

531 Who won Westmeath's first All-Star award in 2001?

532 Who captained Sligo to the 2007 Connacht senior football title?

533 Who managed Dublin to the 1992 All-Ireland final?

534 Sligo footballer Eamonn O'Hara plays for which club?

535 Which college holds the record number of All-Ireland colleges titles?

536 How many All-Ireland senior football titles have Wexford won?

537 Who was the first Donegal footballer to win an All-Star?

538 Who scored Clare's winning goal against Cork in the dying seconds of the 1997 Munster semi-final?

539 Who captained Kerry in the 1975 All-Ireland senior final?

540 Ciaran Lyng, who scored seven points for Wexford in the 2007 Leinster semi-final, was a one-time soccer apprentice with which English club?

ANSWERS PAGE 205

CAPTAINS' PARADE

541 Who captained Donegal to their first All-Ireland senior title in 1992?

542 Name the only hurler to captain All-Ireland senior and U-21 hurling winning sides in the same year.

543 Who captained Waterford to their 2002 Munster hurling title?

544 Who captained Offaly to their first All-Ireland hurling title in 1981?

545 Only two players have captained their clubs to successive All-Ireland club titles. Name them.

546 Who captained St Joseph's Doora-Barefield to the 1999 All-Ireland club hurling title?

547 Who captained Laois to their 2003 Leinster football title?

548 Which former Cork hurling manager captained Cork to a National League title in 1981?

549 Name the former Mayo footballer who captained Galway side Salthill/Knocknacarra to the 2006 All-Ireland club football title.

550 Only two players have captained their county to successive All-Ireland U-21 football titles. Name them.

ANSWERS PAGE 205

551 Only four players have captained successive Fitzgibbon Cup winning teams but one player managed it in the last 10 years. Who was he?

552 Five players have captained their county to successive National Hurling League titles but only one has done so in the last 25 years. Name him.

553 Who captained Antrim in the 1989 All-Ireland senior hurling final?

554 Who captained Tyrone in the 1995 All-Ireland senior football final?

555 What year did Joe Cooney captain Galway in an All-Ireland final?

556 Only two players have captained successive All-Ireland U-21 winning hurling teams, but which one managed it in the last ten years?

557 Two brothers captained Kilkenny to successive All-Ireland U-21 titles in 1974 and 1975. Name them.

558 Name the only two brothers to captain All-Ireland club winning teams.

559 Who was the first player to captain his county to three All-Ireland senior football titles?

560 Who are the only father and son to captain All-Ireland senior winning teams in either hurling or football?

TROPHY PARADE

561 The Bob O'Keeffe Cup is presented annually for what competition?

562 What is the name of the cup presented to the All-Ireland minor hurling champions?

563 The Croke Cup is presented to the winners of what hurling championship?

564 What is the name of the cup presented to the All-Ireland minor football champions?

565 The Tommy Moore Cup is presented to the winners of what hurling championship?

566 What is the name of the cup presented to the Ulster senior football champions?

567 What is the name of the cup presented to the winners of the All-Ireland club football championship?

568 The O'Duffy Cup is presented to the All-Ireland champions of what competition?

569 The Cross of Cashel is presented to which All-Ireland champions?

570 What trophy is presented to the Connacht senior football champions?

ANSWERS PAGE 205

571 The Dr Croke Cup is presented to the winners of what hurling competition?

572 What is the name of the trophy presented to the All-Ireland U-21 football champions?

573 What is the name of the trophy presented to the National Football League champions?

574 The Dan Fraher Cup is presented to the winners of which provincial senior championship?

575 What is the name of the trophy presented to the winners of the International Rules Series?

576 The Liam Harvey Cup is presented to the winners of which provincial senior competition?

577 What is the name of the cup presented to the winners of the Intervarsity camogie championship?

578 The Leinster senior football championship cup didn't have a name until three years ago but what is the name of the trophy now?

579 The Kilcoyne Cup is presented to the winners of which provincial championship each year?

580 What is the name of the Munster senior hurling cup?

ANSWERS PAGE 205

GAA GROUNDS

581 What is the name of the principal GAA County Grounds in Belfast?

582 Where is McHale Park?

583 What is the name of Cavan's county grounds?

584 What is the name of the GAA grounds in Clones?

585 Fraher Field is in what town?

586 Where is Pairc Esler?

587 Name the two counties which are home to Cusack Park?

588 McDonagh Park held a number of National Hurling League games in 2007. Where is it?

589 What is the name of the GAA grounds in Derry City?

590 Where is Healy Park?

591 O'Moore Park is in what town?

592 What is the name of the GAA grounds in Tullamore?

593 MacCumhaill Park is in what town?

594 What is the name of the principal GAA grounds in Armagh City?

ANSWERS PAGE 206

595 What is the name of the GAA Grounds in Carrick-on-Shannon?

596 Where is Dr Cullen Park?

597 What is the name of the GAA ground in Kilkenny city?

598 Where is Pearse Park?

599 Where is Pearse Stadium?

600 McKenna Park held a championship game in the last four years. Where is it?

NATIONAL HURLING LEAGUE

601 When Waterford won the 2007 National Hurling League, how many years had it been since they had won their previous League title?

602 Who captained Waterford to the 2007 League title?

603 The Waterford manager in 2007, Justin McCarthy, had previously won two League titles with which county as a manager?

604 How many League titles have Kilkenny won under Brian Cody?

605 When Kilkenny lost the 2007 League final, it was their first defeat in a League final since what year?

606 What year did Offaly win their only League title?

607 Only one player has managed to captain his county to two League titles in the last ten years. Name him.

608 How many games did Cork play against Wexford to win the 1993 League title?

609 Who captained Galway to the 2004 League title?

610 Diarmuid O'Sullivan captained Cork to a League title in which year?

611 How many League titles did Clare win in the 1990s?

612 Who heads the League roll of honour?

613 Name the only county to win more than three League titles in a row.

614 The 2007 League final failed to produce a goal. The last time a League final failed to produce a goal (it happened in the last 15 years) was in what year?

615 When did Limerick last win a League title?

616 Diarmuid Healy, Canon Michael O'Brien, Michael 'Babs' Keating, Mattie Murphy and Tom Ryan all led their counties to League titles in the 1990s but what was the unusual trend for those managers after their success?

617 When did Wexford last win a National League title?

618 The highest individual score recorded in a League final was in 1960 when a Cork player scored 3-4 in the decider against Tipperary. Name him.

619 Name the player who scored 2-6 for Galway in the 1987 League final against Clare.

620 Only four players have managed to score a total of 12 points or more in League finals but one player has managed that feat twice in the last ten years. Name him.

NICKNAMES

621 James Fitzpatrick (Kilkenny hurler)

622 Kieran Donaghy (Kerry footballer)

623 Michael Walsh (Waterford hurler)

624 Diarmuid Lyng (Wexford hurler)

625 Colm Cooper (Kerry footballer)

626 Gareth Johnson (Down hurler)

627 Jason Sherlock (Dublin footballer)

628 David O'Connor (Wexford hurler)

629 Pat Collier (Meath footballer)

630 John Joe Doyle (Clare hurler)

631 Michael McGrath (Galway hurler)

632 Terence McNaughton (Antrim hurler)

633 Phil Larkin (Kilkenny hurler)

634 Tommy Murphy (Laois footballer)

635 John McGrath (Westmeath hurler)

636 John Mackey (Limerick hurler)

637 Des Fergusson (Dublin footballer)

638 Phil Brady (Cavan footballer)

639 Paddy Brosnan (Kerry footballer)

640 Dick Walsh (Kilkenny hurler)

ANSWERS PAGE 206

CONNACHT FOOTBALL

641 Who scored the winning point for Mayo in the 2006 Connacht final?

642 Prior to 2007, when did Sligo last win a Connacht title?

643 Who scored the winning goal for Roscommon deep in injury time of the 2001 Connacht final?

644 What year did Leitrim last contest a Connacht final?

645 How many Connacht titles did John Maughan win as Mayo manager?

646 Which county holds the record for the greatest number of Connacht senior titles?

647 Who captained Roscommon to the 2001 Connacht title?

648 There was only one goal scored in the 2003 Connacht final between Galway and Mayo. Who scored it?

649 Who scored Mayo's only goal in the 2001 Connacht final?

650 Name the Mayo forward who kicked five points from play (to end as the joint top scorer on the day) in the 1999 Connacht final against Galway.

651 Name the last county to win four Connacht titles in a row.

ANSWERS PAGE 206

652 Leitrim reached four Connacht finals in a row between 1957 and 1960. Which county beat them in every one of those finals?

653 How many Connacht senior championship titles did Tony McManus win with Roscommon?

654 Who did Galway defeat in the 1995 Connacht final?

655 Name the Galway midfielder who kicked four points from play in the 2003 Connacht final.

656 Who scored the only goal in the 1998 replayed Connacht final between Galway and Roscommon?

657 Who kicked a monstrous injury-time equalising point from a long-range placed ball for Roscommon in the 1991 Connacht final?

658 Who captained Galway to the 1995 Connacht title?

659 Who managed Mayo to the 1993 Connacht title?

660 How many Connacht titles has John O'Mahony won as a manager?

GENERAL KNOWLEDGE

661 Martin McHugh managed what county to an Ulster senior title in the 1990s?

662 Which Kerry referee took charge of three All-Ireland football finals between 1988 and 1994?

663 What year was the first 80-minute All-Ireland senior football final?

664 What year was the first 70-minute All-Ireland senior football final?

665 Only five clubs have managed to reach successive All-Ireland club hurling finals. Name them.

666 Seamus Moynihan won Sigerson Cup medals with two different colleges. Name them.

667 Name the Wexford college that reached All-Ireland hurling and football college finals over the last 15 years.

668 Name the dual player who has the most All-Star awards with seven (two football and five hurling).

669 Where is the Palatine GAA club?

670 How many All-Ireland club hurling finals have Athenry appeared in?

671 What year did Lavey win the All-Ireland club football title?

672 There are two Corofin GAA clubs in the country. One is in Galway, where is the second?

673 Only three men have captained their province to successive Interprovincial football titles. John J O'Reilly (Cavan), Paddy Meegan and John O'Keeffe (Kerry) were the three men but which Leinster county did Meegan play for?

674 Who are the only Laois club to win an All-Ireland club title?

675 Horsewood is a GAA club in what county?

676 Who managed Athenry to three All-Ireland club titles?

677 Who were the last Limerick club to reach a Munster club football final in 2002?

678 Sean Guiry managed The Nire to the 2006 Munster club football final but what 2007 inter-county manager trained that team?

679 What was the nickname of the legendary Cork trainer Jim Barry?

680 Who were the last county to win the Oireachtas Hurling Tournament in 2000?

HURLERS IN ALL-IRELAND FINALS IN THE LAST 15 YEARS

Match the hurler to his county

681 Paudie Mulhaire

682 Sean Dowling

683 Ken O'Shea

684 Stephen McNamara

685 Liam McGrath

686 Gary Laffan

687 Cathal Casey

688 Alan Neville

689 Thomas Costello

690 John Reddan

691 Murt Killilea

692 Shane McGuckian

693 Colm Kehoe

694 Liam Burke

695 Ken Coogan

696 Pat Buckley

697 Greg Kennedy

698 Kevin Murray

699 Brendan Kelly

700 Paul Cooney

ANSWERS PAGE 207

GENERAL KNOWLEDGE

701 Who captained Athenry to their first All-Ireland club hurling title in 1997?

702 Name the only father and son from Tyrone to win All-Star awards.

703 Who managed the Kerry hurlers in the 1990s, the Cork minors to an All-Ireland title in 2001 and the Wexford hurlers in 2007?

704 Name the Offaly hurler who won All-Star awards as a defender and a forward.

705 Who captained Birr to their fourth All-Ireland club title in 2004?

706 The former GAA President Paddy McFlynn represented which county?

707 Who was voted GPA Footballer of the Year in 2004, even though his county didn't even qualify for the last 12 of the championship?

708 What club does Kilkenny's Eddie Brennan play for?

709 Name the only Meath player to win All-Stars as a defender and as a forward.

710 Former Tipperary goalkeeper and goalkeeper on the GAA's Hurling Team of the Millennium, Tony Reddan, was a native of which county?

711 When did Monaghan last win an Ulster senior football title?

712 Who won the 2004 All-Ireland minor football title?

713 Name the only two Galway hurlers to have won five All-Stars.

714 Which county won the 1997 All-Ireland U-21 football title?

715 Name the Monaghan player who won All-Stars as a defender and as a forward.

716 Name the Waterford football manager in 2007?

717 Name the Offaly player who hit 1-12 in the 2007 Leinster hurling quarter-final against Laois, a feat which saw him raise more flags (13) than any other Offaly player in a single championship game.

718 Name the only father and son to have won All-Star football awards for different counties in different provinces.

719 Justin McCarthy coached which Ulster team to All-Ireland success in 1970?

720 In what way can Wicklow lay some claim to the 1902 All-Ireland football title?

ANSWERS PAGE 207

PROVINCIAL AND ALL-IRELAND CLUB FOOTBALL CHAMPIONSHIPS OVER THE LAST 20 YEARS

721 Name the only Wicklow club to have won an All-Ireland club title.

722 Current Kerry football manager Pat O'Shea won an All-Ireland club football title with which club?

723 Name the former Galway goalkeeper who played in the 1991 and 2006 All-Ireland club finals with Salthill and Salthill/Knocknacarra.

724 Which club reached three successive Leinster club finals between 1999 and 2001?

725 Who captained Nemo Rangers to the 2003 All-Ireland club title?

726 Who were the last Leinster club to win the All-Ireland club title?

727 What Clare club contested consecutive Munster club finals in 1998 and 1999?

728 Who are the only Down club to win an All-Ireland club title?

729 What club won five Leinster club titles in the 1990s?

ANSWERS PAGE 207

730 What club lost four All-Ireland club finals in a row between 1987 and 1990?

731 An Tochar lost the 1995 Leinster club final after a replay. From which county did they hail?

732 Name the Clare club who won the 2004 Munster club title?

733 Who did Crossmaglen Rangers beat in the 1997 All-Ireland club final?

734 Name the Waterford club that lost the 2004 Munster club final after a replay.

735 When was the last time an All-Ireland club final failed to produce a goal?

736 John Meyler captained which club to an All-Ireland club football title in 1987?

737 Who captained Ballina Stephenites to the 2005 All-Ireland club title?

738 Who did Corofin defeat in the 1998 All-Ireland club final?

739 Four people have played in an All-Ireland club final and also managed a team in an All-Ireland club final over the last 15 years. Name them.

740 Name the three players who captained their club and county to All-Ireland senior titles in the same season.

ALL-IRELAND FOOTBALL FINALS IN THE LAST 15 YEARS

741 Prior to 2007, when was the last drawn All-Ireland final?

742 Name the referee who sent off two players in the 1996 replayed All-Ireland final between Meath and Mayo?

743 Prior to 2007, when was the last time an All-Ireland final failed to produce a goal?

744 Who captained Meath in the 2001 All-Ireland final?

745 Who scored Meath's only goal in the 1999 final?

746 Who captained Down to the 1994 All-Ireland title?

747 Who was the Meath goalkeeper in the 1996 All-Ireland final?

748 How many All-Ireland finals did Dublin contest between 1992 and 1995 inclusive?

749 Which Tyrone player was selected as the RTE Man of the Match in the 2005 All-Ireland final?

750 Who captained Mayo in consecutive All-Ireland finals in 1996 and 1997?

751 Who managed Dublin to the 1995 All-Ireland title?

752 Who captained Derry to the 1993 All-Ireland title?

753 Who managed Down to the 1994 All-Ireland title?

754 Who scored the winning point for Meath in the 1996 All-Ireland final replay?

755 Who were the two Cork goalscorers in the 1993 All-Ireland final?

756 Name the only Kerry player who started in the county's five All-Ireland finals (including one replay) between 1997 and 2004.

757 Who was the Kildare referee who controversially sent off Tony Davis in the 1993 All-Ireland final?

758 Kerry played in five All-Ireland finals (including one replay) between 1997 and 2004 but they only scored one goal in those five games. Name the goalscorer.

759 In the last 15 years (excluding 2007) four players have captained their county in two All-Ireland finals. Name them.

760 In the last 15 years (excluding 2007), only two players have scored goals in two All-Ireland finals. Name them.

CAMOGIE AND LADIES' FOOTBALL FROM THE LAST 15 YEARS

CAMOGIE

761 Which county won the 2006 All-Ireland title?

762 Which two counties clashed in five All-Ireland finals in a row between 2002 and 2006?

763 What year did Tipperary win their first All-Ireland senior title?

764 What year did Galway win their first All-Ireland senior title?

765 Name the last county to win three All-Irelands in a row.

766 What year did the Camogie Association celebrate its Centenary Year?

767 Who tops the All-Ireland senior camogie roll of honour?

768 Angela and Ann Downey hold the record for the third highest number of All-Ireland medals won (12). What year did they win their last All-Ireland with Kilkenny?

769 Name the Dublin player who won 15 All-Ireland senior medals.

770 Who is the only player from the last 10 years to be selected on the Camogie Team of the Century?

ANSWERS PAGE 208

LADIES' FOOTBALL

771 Which county won the 2006 All-Ireland title?

772 Which team won the 2005 All-Ireland junior title and managed to reach the 2006 All-Ireland senior final?

773 Which Munster county reached eight All-Ireland finals between 1991 and 2000, winning five titles?

774 What year did Galway win their first All-Ireland?

775 Mayo contested five All-Ireland finals in a row between 1999 and 2003 but how many did they win?

776 Prior to 2007, name the only Ulster county to win an All-Ireland title in the last 15 years.

777 Which Leinster county lost successive All-Ireland finals in 2003 and 2004?

778 What year did Cork reach their first All-Ireland final?

779 Name the Mayo forward who scored the winning goal with just a minute remaining in the 2003 All-Ireland final.

780 Who kicked the winning point for Laois in the dying seconds of the 2001 All-Ireland final to secure Laois their first title?

ANSWERS PAGE 208

ULSTER GENERAL KNOWLEDGE?

781 Name the four Derry clubs that won five Ulster club football titles between 1994 and 2004.

782 Mullaghbawn won an Ulster club football title in the last 15 years but which year?

783 What year did Paul Brewster captain Queen's University to a Sigerson Cup title?

784 Who captained Armagh to the 1999 Ulster senior title?

785 How many Ulster club titles have Crossmaglen won?

786 When was the last time a Down club won the Ulster club hurling championship?

787 Who did Dunloy defeat in the 2004 All-Ireland club hurling semi-final?

788 Who was the last Ulster President of the GAA?

789 Monaghan's Paul Finlay won a Sigerson Cup medal with which college in 2004?

790 Armagh's Enda McNulty won successive Sigerson Cup medals with two different colleges in 2000 and 2001. Name those two colleges.

791 Which county has their training centre at Owenbeg?

792 Who were Armagh's joint managers that led them to the 1999 and 2000 Ulster titles?

793 Donegal's Christy Toye captained which college to Sigerson glory in 2005?

794 Which county has won the most senior provincial football titles?

795 Who managed Down when they reached the 1997 All-Ireland hurling quarter-final?

796 Who captained Armagh to the 2004 All-Ireland U-21 football title?

797 Who did Dunloy defeat in the 2003 All-Ireland club hurling semi-final?

798 Name the Antrim senior football manager in 2007?

799 Name the Armagh footballer who won four Ulster senior football titles and an All-Ireland senior title but who also played Interprovincial hurling for Ulster.

800 When did Fermanagh last appear in an Ulster senior football final?

ANSWERS PAGE 208

FORMER COUNTY FOOTBALLERS AND THEIR CLUBS

801 Mickey Linden (Down)

802 Tony Davis (Cork)

803 Mikey Sheehy (Kerry)

804 John O'Leary (Dublin)

805 Sean Og de Paor (Galway)

806 Eoin Liston (Kerry)

807 Mick Lyons (Meath)

808 Liam McHale (Mayo)

809 Benny Tierney (Armagh)

810 John McDermott (Meath)

811 Anthony Tohill (Derry)

812 Declan O'Keeffe (Kerry)

813 Joe Kernan (Armagh)

814 Niall Cahalane (Cork)

815 Maurice Fitzgerald (Kerry)

816 Joe Kavanagh (Cork)

817 Dara O Cinneide (Kerry)

818 Fergal O'Donnell (Rosscommon)

819 Kevin Walsh (Galway)

820 Kevin O'Brien (Wicklow)

ANSWERS PAGE 208

INTERPROVINCIAL CHAMPIONSHIPS – PLAYERS INVOLVED OVER THE LAST 15 YEARS

821 Who is the current sponsor of the Interprovincial Championships?

822 Niall McCusker was full-back on the Ulster team that won the 2003 title. Which county is he from?

823 Name the Kildare goalkeeper on the successful Leinster football team in 2002.

824 Two Clare defenders captained Munster to hurling success in 1996 and 1997. Name them.

825 Name the current Dublin footballer who won two Interprovincial hurling medals with Leinster in 2002 and 2003.

826 Derek Barrett won a hurling title with Munster in 2000. Which county did he play for?

827 Name the Kildare goalkeeper who won two titles with Leinster in 1996 and 1997.

828 Name the current Limerick forward who played in four Interprovincial hurling finals between 1997 and 2004 as either a defender or midfielder.

829 Cyril Duggan was full-back on the successful Leinster hurling side in 1993. Which county did he play for?

ANSWERS PAGE 208

830 John Hegarty won a title with Leinster footballers in 2001. Which county did he play for?

831 Name the Laois goalkeeper who played for Leinster in the 1997 Interprovincial hurling final.

832 Nicky Horan played wing-forward in the 2000 hurling final for Leinster. Which county did he play for?

833 Niall Smyth played for Ulster on four successful Interprovincial football teams in a row between 1991 and 1994. Which county did he play for?

834 The 2007 Tipperary football manager played in an Interprovincial football final for Munster in 1994. Name him.

835 Ollie Fahy captained which province to Interprovincial success in 2004?

836 Brendan Rouine played corner-back for the Munster footballers in the 1996 final. Which county did he play for?

837 Munster and Leinster contested the 2005 Interprovincial hurling final in which city?

838 Pat Potterton played wing-forward on the successful Leinster hurling team in 1993. Which county did he play for?

839 Alan Malone won a football title with Munster in 1999 at corner-back. Which county did he play for?

840 Name the player who won an Interprovincial hurling title with Connacht in 1994 and an All-Ireland senior medal with Wexford (as a panellist) in 1996.

CONNACHT GENERAL KNOWLEDGE

841 Who won the 2007 Connacht U-21 football title?

842 Who did Sligo beat in the 2007 Connacht championship quarter-final and semi-final?

843 Who did St Brigid's defeat in the 2006 Connacht club football final?

844 Who was the last Connacht man to be GAA President?

845 Name the former Galway goalkeeper who subsequently managed Roscommon against Galway in three Connacht hurling finals.

846 Paul Seevers is a well-known hurler with which county?

847 Who managed NUIG to the 2007 Fitzgibbon Cup final?

848 Which Sligo club contested the 2003 Connacht club football final?

849 How many Connacht counties has John Maughan managed?

850 Who was the Leitrim football manager in 2007?

851 Who were the last county to retain the Connacht senior football title?

852 Name the Roscommon club that contested three Connacht club hurling finals in a row between 2000 and 2002.

853 Which well-known insurance company sponsors the Connacht football league?

854 How many All-Ireland minor hurling finals did Galway contest between 1996 and 2006 (inclusive)?

855 Name the Galway club that reached the 2001 Connacht club football final.

856 Name the Mayo club that contested three Connacht club hurling finals in a row between 1997 and 1999.

857 Name the Galway college that contested All-Ireland colleges hurling and football finals over the last 15 years.

858 What year did the last Connacht hurling final take place?

859 Name the St Brigid's player that scored a sensational last-minute goal to win the 2006 Connacht club football title?

860 Prior to 2007, who were the last Connacht county to win an All-Ireland minor football title?

ANSWERS PAGE 209

ACE OF CLUBS

861 How many Munster club titles have Nemo Rangers won? Eight, ten or thirteen?

862 Birr contested eight Leinster club hurling finals between 1991 and 2006 but how many did they win?

863 Who are the only club to win All-Ireland club titles in both codes?

864 Name the three clubs who won successive All-Ireland club football titles.

865 Three clubs from Cork won seven out of eight All-Ireland club hurling titles between 1972 and 1979. Name those clubs.

866 Name the three clubs to win successive All-Ireland club hurling titles.

867 Name the club that won six Connacht club football titles in a row in the 1980s.

868 Name the two clubs that have won four All-Ireland club hurling titles.

869 Which Kilkenny club have won three All-Ireland club hurling titles?

870 Name the Tipperary club that won ten county titles in an 11-year period between 1955 and 1965.

ANSWERS PAGE 209

871 How many Armagh county titles in a row did Crossmaglen Rangers win between 1996 and 2006 (inclusive)?

872 Name the Waterford club that won nine county hurling titles in a row between 1953 and 1961.

873 Name the only Munster club to reach successive All-Ireland club hurling finals.

874 Name the Tipperary club that won ten county titles in a 15-year period between 1992 and 2006.

875 Who were the first club from Connacht to win an All-Ireland club football title?

876 Name the Kerry club that won successive Munster club football titles in 1995 and 1996.

877 Name the Offaly club that won successive Leinster football titles in 1978 and 1979.

878 Who are the only Tyrone club to have won the Ulster club football title?

879 Name the club that reached six Ulster club football finals in a row in the 1980s, winning five of those finals?

880 How many Ulster club hurling titles did Dunloy Cuchulainns win between 2000 and 2003?

GAA PLAYERS WHO MADE A BIG IMPACT IN THEIR FIRST FULL SEASON?

881 How many goals did Jimmy Barry Murphy score in the 1973 All-Ireland football final?

882 How many goals did Eoin Liston score in his first All-Ireland final in 1978?

883 Name the Kerry 19-year-old who kicked 11 points from Kerry's total of 0-16 in the 1988 Munster football final.

884 Name the young goal scoring forward who ignited Dublin's All-Ireland winning football team in 1995.

885 Name the young rookie forward who ignited Cork's charge to the 2003 All-Ireland hurling final.

886 Name the 19-year-old Armagh full-forward who scored 0-3 from play in the 2002 All-Ireland football final.

887 How many goals did Kieran Donaghy score in the 2006 All-Ireland football final?

888 Tipperary's Eoin Kelly won an All-Star hurling award in his first full season. Which year?

889 Waterford's Eoin Kelly won an All-Star hurling award in his first season. Which season?

890 Name the 19-year-old Galway midfielder who was man of the match in Galway's 2001 All-Ireland hurling semi-final win against Kilkenny.

ANSWERS PAGE 209

891 Name the Clare midfielder who won an All-Star hurling award in his debut season in 1995.

892 Name the Cork player who won 'Hurler of the Year' as a 19-year-old in 1992.

893 Name the Kilkenny player who scored 0-3 from play in the 2003 All-Ireland final and ended with an All-Star in his debut season.

894 Name the goalkeeper who won a hurling All-Star in 1998 in his debut season.

895 Name the Tyrone player who won an All-Star football award in his first full season in 2001.

896 Colm Cooper won an All-Star in his first season as a 19-year-old. Which season?

897 Name the Kerry player selected as Young Footballer of the Year in 1997 after his first season.

898 Padraig Joyce won an All-Star award in his debut season. Which season?

899 Name the Tipperary hurler selected as Young Hurler of the Year in 1997 as a 19-year-old.

900 Name the Mayo player who won a football All-Star award in his first season in 1993.

TRAINERS

901 John McCloskey was the trainer of which All-Ireland senior winning football team over the last ten years?

902 Name the Kerry physical trainer for Kerry's two All-Ireland titles under Jack O'Connor.

903 Seanie McGrath was one of Cork's two trainers for their two All-Ireland hurling titles in 2004 and 2005. Name the second.

904 Paddy Tally trained which All-Ireland senior winning football team over the last ten years and in which year?

905 Mick O'Flynn trained which successful hurling county for over a decade during the last 15 years?

906 Name the four Ulster senior sides that Martin McElkennon has trained in the last ten years.

907 Gerry Dempsey trained which senior hurling team to an All-Ireland final over the last ten years?

908 Prior to 2007, Louis Mulqueen was the trainer of which senior hurling team that reached an All-Ireland final over the last ten years?

909 Name the former Laois footballer who was trainer and selector with Kilkenny for their All-Ireland hurling success in 2006.

910 Dave Mahedy trained which county to two All-Ireland senior hurling finals over the last 15 years?

ANSWERS PAGE 209

911 Who trained Mayo to the 2006 All-Ireland football final?

912 Prior to 2007, Gerry Fitzpatrick trained which county to two All-Ireland hurling semi-finals in the previous five years?

913 Brian Murray trained which county in the hurling championship in 2007?

914 The athletics coach Jim Kilty trained which team to an All-Ireland senior hurling title in the last 10 years?

915 Prior to 2007, who is the only trainer to train two different teams to All-Ireland senior football semi-finals over the previous five years?

916 Name the trainer who trained Cork to Munster senior hurling and football success between 1999 and 2006.

917 Prior to 2007, who is the only trainer to train two different counties to All-Ireland senior hurling finals in the last ten years?

918 Prior to 2007 name the Cork player who scored 3-2 in the 2002 All-Ireland camogie final and who subsequently went on to train the Cork camogie team to two All-Irelands.

919 Name the Tyrone trainer for their 2005 All-Ireland senior title success.

920 Name the trainer who has trained teams to Munster senior hurling and football finals over the last five years.

THE TOP 20 SCORERS IN ALL-IRELAND HURLING FINALS (PRIOR TO 2007)

Note, the players in question are rated by the questions ie 921 is number one and so on?

921 Name the legendary Kilkenny player who scored 7-74 in ten All-Ireland finals.

922 Name the legendary Tipperary player who scored 1-43 in nine finals.

923 Name the legendary Cork player who scored 3-36 in ten finals.

924 Charlie McCarthy from Cork scored 3-35 in how many finals, five, six or seven?

925 DJ Carey scored 4-32 in All-Ireland finals but how many finals did he play in?

926 Prior to 2007, Henry Shefflin was the sixth highest scorer in All-Ireland finals with 2-34 but how many finals had he played in by that stage?

927 Nicky Rackard hit 5-13 in All-Ireland finals but how many finals did he play in?

928 Dave Clohessy scored 8-2 in four All-Ireland finals for which county?

929 Name the former All-Ireland winning selector with Tipperary who hit 6-8 in eight finals.

ANSWERS PAGE 209

930 Liam O'Brien hit 1-22 in five All-Ireland finals for which county?

931 Joe Cooney hit 1-22 in how many All-Ireland final appearances for Galway?

932 Jimmy Langton is the 12th highest scorer in All-Ireland finals with 0-25 but which county did he play for?

933 Name the Tipperary player from the last 20 years who has the second best average in All-Ireland finals with an average of 0-8.

934 In PJ Molloy's last three All-Ireland final appearances for Galway in 1985, 1986 and 1987, he scored a goal in two of those three finals. Which two years did he score those goals?

935 Kilkenny's Billy Fitzpatrick scored 1-19 in six All-Ireland final appearances but in which final did he hit 0-10?

936 Padge Kehoe scored 2-16 in six finals for which county?

937 Joe Deane hit 0-22 in five All-Ireland finals but how many of those points were from play. Three, five or seven?

938 Seanie O'Leary hit 5-6 for Cork in how many final appearances?

939 Tom Walsh scored 5-5 for Kilkenny in four All-Ireland final appearances but in which final did Walsh lose an eye, an injury which subsequently ended his career?

940 Name the Cork forward who hit 4-8 in six finals between 1982 and 1992.

MUNSTER GENERAL KNOWLEDGE

941 Who scored the late equalising goal for Limerick in their first drawn Munster hurling semi-final against Tipperary in 2007?

942 Name the Limerick forward who scored ten points from play and who set up their two goals in the first and second drawn Munster hurling semi-finals against Tipperary in 2007?

943 Name the Cork forward who scored 3-14 in their 2007 Munster football quarter-final and semi-final wins against Limerick and Tipperary.

944 Who did Newtownshandrum defeat in the 2005 Munster club hurling final?

945 Which club does Kerry's Paul Galvin play for?

946 Who managed the Limerick footballers in 2006 and 2007?

947 Which Clare club contested two Munster club football finals in the last five years?

948 Name the four Clare clubs that won six provincial hurling titles in a row between 1995 and 2000.

949 Name the Waterford hurling goalkeeper for their two Munster senior hurling titles in 2002 and 2004.

950 Prior to 2007, who were the last Munster county to win an All-Ireland minor football title and what was the year?

951 Name the Tipperary hurling goalkeeper who made his debut in the 2007 second drawn Munster senior hurling semi-final against Limerick.

952 Who captained Cork to the 2006 Munster football title?

953 When did Clare last win a Munster senior hurling championship game?

954 When Limerick defeated Tipperary after the second replay of the 2007 Munster hurling semi-final they won a Munster championship game for the first time since what year?

955 When did the Kerry hurlers last play in the Munster hurling championship?

956 Prior to 2007, who were the last Limerick club to contest a Munster club hurling final?

957 Prior to 2007, who were the last county to win Munster U-21 hurling and football titles in the same season?

958 Cork only had three players sent off in Championship hurling in the last 40 years. Who was the most recent?

959 Name the Waterford goalscorers in their 5-15 to 3-18 Munster hurling semi-final win over Cork in 2007.

960 Six St Finbarr's (Cork) clubmen have managed or trained inter-county senior hurling teams over the last 20 years. Name them.

ANSWERS PAGE 210

CLUBCALL 2

Name the county of the following clubs

961 Ballyhea

962 Ballyduff Lower

963 Dromid Pearses

964 Ballyea

965 Ballycran

966 Drom-Inch

967 Murroe-Boher

968 Mullahoran

969 Craughwell

970 Aughavas

971 Athleague

972 Cuala

973 Clonduff

974 Raharney

975 Cloughbawn

976 Trillick

977 Eastern Harps

978 Timahoe

979 Lisnaskea

980 Knockbridge

ANSWERS PAGE 210

GENERAL KNOWLEDGE

981 When did Derry last contest an Ulster football final?

982 Who captained Offaly to the 1982 All-Ireland football title?

983 What Kilkenny club is known as 'The Village'?

984 Where is Duggan Park?

985 Which Dublin club won the 2005 Leinster club football championship?

986 Who captained Dr Crokes to the 2007 All-Ireland club football final?

987 Name the college that Kilkenny hurler JJ Delaney captained to a Fitzgibbon Cup title in 2004.

988 Who managed the Wexford footballers in 2006 and 2007?

989 Who managed the Antrim hurlers to the 2006 Christy Ring Cup title?

990 Prior to 2007, who were the last county to suffer back to back defeats in All-Ireland senior football semi-finals?

991 Who managed Tipperary to the 1997 All-Ireland hurling final?

992 In which city is the club Steelstown?

993 Name the former Donegal footballer who captained two different Sigerson Cup winning teams (IT Tralee and UUJ) in the last ten years.

994 Which Monaghan club won three Ulster club titles in a row between 1978 and 1980?

995 Who was the last player to score goals in successive years in Ulster football finals?

996 Which are the only parish (two clubs drawing their players from the same area) to contest provincial finals in hurling and football over the last decade?

997 Name the Tyrone player who scored goals in successive Ulster football finals in 1994 and 1995.

998 What year did Longford win their only Leinster senior football title?

999 Who is the only Offaly hurler to have won three All-Ireland senior medals?

1000 Who is the only Offaly footballer to have won three All-Ireland senior medals?

ANSWERS PAGE 210

MANAGERIAL ROLL CALL

1001 Who managed Roscommon to the 2006 All-Ireland minor football title?

1002 Who managed Westmeath to the 1995 All-Ireland minor football title?

1003 How many All-Ireland minor hurling titles did Mattie Murphy win as Galway manager between 1992 and 2006 (he wasn't manager for all of those years)?

1004 Who managed Mayo to the 2006 All-Ireland U-21 football title?

1005 Who managed Kilkenny to the 2003 All-Ireland U-21 title?

1006 Who managed Tipperary to the 2006 All-Ireland minor title?

1007 Mark Turley managed which team to All-Ireland football success in 2005?

1008 Who managed Galway to successive All-Ireland minor titles in 1999 and 2000?

1009 Maurice Aylward managed which team to All-Ireland success in 2007?

1010 How many All-Ireland minor titles did Mickey Harte win with Tyrone?

ANSWERS PAGE 210

1011 Who managed Cork to the 2007 All-Ireland U-21 football title?

1012 What team did Eoin O'Donnellan manage to All-Ireland success in 2006?

1013 What team did Jody Gormley manage to All-Ireland success in 2006?

1014 What team did Sean Treacy manage to All-Ireland hurling success in 2006?

1015 Who managed the Carlow team that reached the 2006 Christy Ring Cup final?

1016 Who managed Westmeath to the 2005 Christy Ring title?

1017 Name the former Kildare footballer who managed Moorefield to the 2006 Leinster club title.

1018 Mick O'Dea managed what team to success in what competition in 2005?

1019 Who managed Wicklow to the 2007 Division Two National hurling league final?

1020 Who managed Loughrea to the 2007 All-Ireland club hurling final?

ANSWERS PAGE 210

GAA AUTOBIOGRAPHIES

Name the GAA stars who wrote the following books

1021 *Out Of Our Skins*

1022 *Raising The Banner*

1023 *Dessie, Tangled Up In Blue*

1024 *Passion And Pride*

1025 *Kicking Down Heavens Door*

1026 *Triumph And Troubles*

1027 *Shooting From The Hip*

1028 *I Crossed The Line*

1029 *The Earley Years*

1030 *All Or Nothing*

1031 *Back To The Hill*

1032 *The Final Whistle*

1033 *Hooked*

1034 *Misunderstood*

1035 *Every Single Ball*

1036 *The Right To Win*

1037 *To Hell And Back*

1038 *Beyond The Tunnel*

1039 *Keys To The Kingdom*

1040 *The Gambler*

ANSWERS PAGE 211

HURLING GENERAL KNOWLEDGE

1041 Who captained Kilkenny to the 2005 National Hurling League title?

1042 Name the Cork player who scored goals on both days against Clare and Waterford in the 2007 Munster hurling quarter and semi-final.

1043 Who was Clare's only hurling All-Star in 2006?

1044 Name the former All-Star defender who scored two goals for Wexford in the 2001 drawn All-Ireland semi-final.

1045 Who scored two goals for Cork in the 2007 Munster hurling semi-final against Waterford?

1046 Who captained Offaly to the 1994 All-Ireland title?

1047 Name John Mullane's club.

1048 Which year did Sixmilebridge win the All-Ireland club title?

1049 Who captained Wexford to the 1996 All-Ireland senior title?

1050 When did Clare last contest a Munster senior hurling final?

1051 Which Leinster team contested the 2005 Nicky Rackard Cup final?

1052 Which year did Kiltormer win the All-Ireland club hurling title?

ANSWERS PAGE 211

1053 Name Joe Deane's club.

1054 Who captained Offaly in the 1995 All-Ireland senior final?

1055 Who managed Limerick to All-Ireland senior finals in 1994 and 1996?

1056 Eoin Kelly from Tipperary had a penalty saved in the 2005 Munster hurling final but name the goalkeeper who saved it.

1057 In the last ten years, Kilkenny twice won All-Ireland minor and senior hurling titles in the same year. Name both of those seasons.

1058 Who managed the Offaly hurlers to the 2004 Leinster final?

1059 Mick Gill won All-Ireland hurling medals with two different counties within three months of each other in 1924. The 1923 All-Ireland final was played in September and the 1924 final was played two months later. There was no declaration rule in operation then so name the two counties Gill won All-Irelands with.

1060 Who scored Limerick's goal from a penalty in the 1980 All-Ireland hurling final

LEINSTER HURLING FINALS

1061 Who captained Wexford to the 2004 Leinster hurling title?

1062 Of the 11 Leinster hurling finals between 1980 and 1990 (inclusive), how many did Offaly contest?

1063 How many Leinster titles did Offaly win between 1980 and 1990 (inclusive)?

1064 How many Leinster finals did Wexford and Kilkenny contest against each other between 2001 and 2007 (inclusive)?

1065 Who scored Kilkenny's only goal in the 2006 Leinster final?

1066 When was the last time a Leinster final failed to produce a goal?

1067 What year did Dublin last contest a Leinster final?

1068 Which Wexford player was top scorer in the 2002 Leinster final with 0-13?

1069 Name the player who got man-of-the-match in the 1997 Leinster final even though he was only on the pitch for the last 15 minutes.

1070 What year did Laois last contest a Leinster final?

1071 Who was the Offaly goalkeeper for the 1994 Leinster final?

1072 Michael Bond managed Offaly in how many Leinster finals?

1073 What year did Dublin last win a Leinster title?

1074 What year did Laois last win a Leinster title?

1075 When did the Leinster final last end in a draw?

1076 Who was the Offaly goalkeeper for the 1996 Leinster final?

1077 How many Leinster SHC titles did DJ Carey win?

1078 What year did Damien Fitzhenry play in his first Leinster senior final?

1079 What year in the 1990s did Johnny Dooley play in a Leinster final for Kilkenny?

1080 Who was the only Kilkenny player to play in their six Leinster title winning teams in a row between 1998 and 2003?

ANSWERS PAGE 211

FOOTBALLERS AND THEIR CLUBS 1

Name the club of the following footballers

1081 Steven McDonnell (Armagh)

1082 Tom Brewster (Fermanagh)

1083 Ray Cosgrove (Dublin)

1084 Michael Meehan (Galway)

1085 Matty Forde (Wexford)

1086 Benny Coulter (Down)

1087 Conor John McGourty (Antrim)

1088 Peadar Gardiner (Mayo)

1089 John Galvin (Limerick)

1090 Ross Munnelly (Laois)

1091 Brian Dooher (Tyrone)

1092 Niall McNamee (Offaly)

1093 Paul Barden (Longford)

1094 Kevin Cassidy (Donegal)

1095 Darren Fay (Meath)

1096 Graham Canty (Cork)

1097 Paddy Bradley (Derry)

1098 Declan Browne (Tipperary)

1099 John Doyle (Kildare)

1100 Dessie Dolan (Westmeath)

ANSWERS PAGE 211

COUNTY SWITCHERS

Name the county that the following players switched their allegiance to

1101 Rory Gallagher (Fermanagh)

1102 Andy Maloney (Tipperary)

1103 Shea Fahy (Kildare)

1104 Declan Darcy (Leitrim)

1105 Brian Flannery (Tipperary)

1106 Mark Mullins (Carlow)

1107 Karl O'Dwyer (Kerry)

1108 Denis Byrne (Kilkenny)

1109 Brian Lacey (Tipperary)

1110 Billy Sheehan (Kerry)

1111 Tomas Tierney (Galway)

1112 Shane King (Fermanagh)

1113 Stephen Mulvenna (Antrim)

1114 Garvan Ware (Carlow)

1115 Niall Geary (Waterford)

1116 PJ Ward (Westmeath)

1117 Mossie Carroll (Limerick)

1118 Eamonn Morrissey (Kilkenny)

1119 Thomas Walsh (Carlow)

1120 Maurice Horan (Mayo)

ANSWERS PAGE 212

GENERAL KNOWLEDGE

1121 With which county did the comedian Patrick Kielty win an All-Ireland minor medal?

1122 Who was the only modern Galway player (from their All-Ireland winning teams of 1998 and 2001) to be selected on the Galway Football Team of the Millennium?

1123 Six modern Clare players (from their All-Ireland winning teams of 1995 and 1997) were selected on the Clare Hurling Team of the Millennium. Name five of them.

1124 Who was Armagh's first All-Star?

1125 Name the two Cork captains (hurling and football) who led their sides to the double in 1990.

1126 Kerry were 90 seconds away from a nine-in a row of Munster football titles in 1983 when a Cork substitute scored a goal to give his side a one-point win. Name the scorer.

1127 Where was the 1983 All-Ireland semi-final replay between Dublin and Cork played?

1128 Who captained Wexford to the 2005 National Football League final?

1129 Who managed Westmeath to their first All-Ireland U-21 football title in 1999?

1130 Name the hurling goalkeeper who scored a point from a free in an All-Ireland senior semi-final in 1982.

ANSWERS PAGE 212

1131 Which former professional snooker player played for Cosiland Na Fianna?

1132 He was a midfielder on the Kildare team that won the 1919 All-Ireland football title and he also played on the 1923 All-Ireland winning Dublin team. He also competed with the Irish Olympic team of 1924 in the high jump. Name him.

1133 Between 1988 and 1996, six players were sent off in All-Ireland football finals. Name them.

1134 Name the only Waterford player selected on the GAA's Hurling Team of the Millennium.

1135 Name the only Cavan player selected on the GAA's Football Team of the Millennium.

1136 Name the only Limerick player selected on the GAA's Hurling Team of the Millennium.

1137 Name the only Down player selected on the GAA's Football Team of the Millennium.

1138 Only one modern player from the last ten years was selected on the Munster Hurling Team of the Millennium. He was a defender. Name him.

1139 Which club contested All-Ireland club hurling and football finals in the same year in 1981?

1140 How many All-Ireland club hurling finals did Dunloy contest between 1995 and 2004?

ANSWERS PAGE 212

COUNTY NICKNAMES

Match the county to the nickname

1141 The Rebels

1142 The Saffrons

1143 The Breffni

1144 The Oakleaf

1145 The Lilywhites

1146 The Mourne County

1147 The Royals

1148 The Premier

1149 The O'Moore County

1150 The Faithful

1151 The Model County

1152 The Farney

1153 Yeats County

1154 The Lake County

1155 The Orchard County

1156 The Garden County

1157 The Shannonsiders

1158 The O'Donnell County

1159 The O'Neill County

1160 The Scallion Eaters

ANSWERS PAGE 212

GENERAL KNOWLEDGE

1161 Who was the Galway goalkeeper in the 2001 All-Ireland football final?

1162 In what year was the 'Thunder and Lightning' All-Ireland hurling final?

1163 What year did Paidi O Se captain Kerry to an All-Ireland senior title?

1164 Who was the former All-Ireland winning senior football captain and All-Ireland senior football final referee who was known as the 'The Man in the Cap'?

1165 Who captained Down to the 1991 All-Ireland senior football title?

1166 What club does Armagh's Paul McGrane play for?

1167 Between 1996 and 2006, two men each refereed three All-Ireland senior football finals. Name them.

1168 Who refereed four All-Ireland hurling finals between 1992 and 1998?

1169 Name the three Kerry footballers who won four All-Ireland senior medals between 1997 and 2006.

1170 What club does Clare's Niall Gilligan play for?

1171 Who captained Cork to the 1989 All-Ireland football title?

1172 Kilkenny contested four All-Ireland U-21 hurling finals between 2003 and 2006 but how many did they win?

1173 Who won the 2007 All-Ireland Colleges football title?

1174 What club does Tyrone's Conor Gormley play for?

1175 In the last 20 years, which four Meath players have won All-Ireland minor, U-21 and senior medals on the field of play?

1176 Which club won the 2006 Ulster club hurling title?

1177 It took three games to separate Limerick and Tipperary in the 2007 Munster championship but when was the previous occasion when three games were needed to separate two teams in the hurling championship (it happened in the last ten years)?

1178 An inter-county hurling goalkeeper scored 0-7 from frees in a club championship game in 2007, even though he was still playing in goal. Name him.

1179 Name the father and son combination who made their managerial and championship starting debuts on the same day with the same county in the 2007 football championship.

1180 Three Cork hurling captains have been substituted in All-Ireland finals over the last 15 years. Name all three.

ANSWERS PAGE 212

HURLING ALL-STARS

1181 What year did Sean Og and Setanta O hAilpin win All-Star awards?

1182 Two modern Clare hurlers (from the 1995 and 1997 All-Ireland winning teams) hold the record number of All-Star awards (4) for their county. Name them.

1183 Who has the greatest number of hurling All-Stars?

1184 How many All-Stars did Noel Skehan win?

1185 Prior to 2007, Dublin won their last hurling All-Star in 1990. Name that player.

1186 Name the goalkeeper who won three All-Stars between 1977 and 1981, even though his county never won a provincial title in that time.

1187 Name the only twins to win All-Stars.

1188 Who won Down's first and only All-Star?

1189 Who was Galway's first All-Star?

1190 Name the player who won three All-Stars in a row between 1983 and 1985 even though his county didn't even win a provincial title in that time.

1191 Who won Laois' first and only All-Star?

ANSWERS PAGE 213

1192 Name the Cork hurler who won five All-Stars between 1982 and 1992.

1193 What player was voted Hurler of the Year yet didn't receive an All-Star award?

1194 Who won Westmeath's first and only All-Star?

1195 What year did the late Tommy Quaid win an All-Star award as a goalkeeper?

1196 Prior to 2007, six sets of brothers have won All-Stars in the last ten years. Name those sets of brothers.

1197 Brian Corcoran won All-Star awards in how many different positions?

1198 Name the only Limerick hurler to win six All-Stars.

1199 Name the two Galway brothers who won a combined seven All-Stars between them.

1200 Three sets of three brothers have won All-Stars. Name them.

ANSWERS PAGE 213

ULSTER FOOTBALL FINALS

1201 Prior to 2007, when was the last time a final ended in a draw?

1202 What year did Cavan last reach an Ulster final?

1203 How many Ulster titles did Armagh win between 1999 and 2006?

1204 How many Ulster finals did Tyrone contest between 2001 and 2007 (inclusive)?

1205 Name the player who scored 2-7 in the 1999 Ulster final.

1206 Name the player who only touched the ball seven times but who scored 2-1 in the 2003 Ulster final.

1207 When Tyrone won consecutive Ulster titles in 1995 and 1996, they became the first county to win back-to-back Ulster titles since 1976. Who were the last county to achieve that feat?

1208 When Armagh won three Ulster titles in a row between 2004 and 2006, they became the first county in over 40 years to achieve that feat. Who were the last county to do so?

1209 Who scored the only goal in the 1998 Ulster final between Derry and Donegal?

1210 What significant landmark did Oisin McConville achieve during the 2006 Ulster final?

ANSWERS PAGE 213

1211 Who scored the only goal in the 2006 Ulster final between Armagh and Donegal?

1212 Who captained Tyrone to the 2001 Ulster title?

1213 How many Ulster finals did Donegal contest between 1996 and 2006?

1214 Who did Tyrone defeat in the 1995 final to win their first title in six years?

1215 Who managed Monaghan to the 2007 Ulster final?

1216 How many Ulster titles did Peter Canavan win with Tyrone?

1217 Who captained Cavan to the 1997 Ulster title?

1218 Name the Armagh forward who was top scorer from play in the 2004 final with 1-3.

1219 When did Antrim last contest an Ulster final, 1970, 1975 or 1980?

1220 Name the Derry forward who was top scorer in the 2000 final with 1-3.

CONTROVERSIES

1221 What was the name of the referee who blew the final whistle two minutes early in the 1998 All-Ireland hurling semi-final replay between Clare and Offaly?

1222 The Cork hurling captain in 2007 Kieran Murphy (Erins Own) received two yellow cards in the 2000 All-Ireland minor football semi-final but wasn't sent off and was the most influential player on the pitch in the last 20 minutes as Cork progressed to the final. Who did Cork beat in that semi-final?

1223 Rule 27 of the GAA Rule book, which prohibited GAA members from playing, attending or promoting rugby, soccer, hockey or cricket, was in place for 67 years until its abolition in 1971. What was the rule known as?

1224 Which Rule, which precluded members of the British Army and Royal Ulster Constabulary from becoming members of the GAA, was abolished in 2001?

1225 Name the four players who were sent off in the 1983 All-Ireland football final.

1226 In the 1995 Leinster championship, Laois won their Leinster quarter-final by a point but a point by Laois forward Leo Turley was shown to have been wide on TV. Laois offered a replay to which team?

1227 Name the player who was at the centre of a huge suspension controversy before the 1989 All-Ireland hurling semi-final between Galway and Tipperary.

1228 Name the Cork footballer who was judged to be harshly sent off in the 1993 All-Ireland football final.

1229 Name the hurler who was controversially suspended for three months on video evidence after the 1998 replayed Munster final.

1230 Name the two players sent off in the 1996 replayed All-Ireland football final after a mass brawl at the beginning of the game.

1231 Before the 1976 Munster football final, Cork became involved in an Adidas jersey sponsorship deal which became known as what affair?

1232 Which year did the Cork hurlers famously go 'on strike'?

1233 Name the referee who sent off those four players in the 1983 All-Ireland football final.

1234 Before the 1956 All-Ireland hurling final, four players walked off in protest at their paltry ticket allocation. The players were from which county?

1235 Although the GAA later ruled the deal out of order, a week before the 1985 All-Ireland final, the Kerry squad stripped off and posed beside a washing machine to promote that company's product. What was the name of the washing machine company at the heart of the controversy?

1236 What was the name of the company that paid four players €750 each to display their logo on their hurleys during the 2003 All-Ireland hurling semi-final?

1237 Name the Crossmaglen player who received two yellow cards in the 2007 All-Ireland club final replay but who wasn't sent off.

1238 Name six of the seven Cork and Clare players who were suspended arising out of incidents prior to the 2007 Cork-Clare Munster hurling semi-final.

1239 When the Clanna Gael Fontenoys GAA club in south Dublin came up with a novel fund-raising plan in 1991 to stage a Gaelic football game between Dublin and Down and a soccer match between Dublin rivals Shamrock Rovers and Bohemians, it turned into one of the decade's biggest sporting controversies. What was the affair known as?

1240 An All-Ireland senior hurling final was won only once on a walkover. In what year?

FOOTBALLERS WHO HAVE PLAYED IN ALL-IRELAND FINALS OVER THE LAST 15 YEARS

Match the county to the player

1241 Podsie O'Mahony

1242 Ray Magee

1243 Aodhan Mac Gearailt

1244 Fergal Costello

1245 John Madden

1246 Enda Gormley

1247 Keith Galvin

1248 John Cullinane

1249 Gary Mason

1250 Barry Moran

1251 Kieran Hughes

1252 Joe McMahon

1253 Brendan Guiney

1254 Ray Dempsey

1255 Joyce McMullan

1256 Jimmy McGuinness

1257 Denis O'Dwyer

1258 Billy O'Shea

1259 Shay Walsh

1260 Fergal Kelly

ANSWERS PAGE 213

FAMOUS GAA FAMILIES

1261 Name the three brothers who won an All-Ireland hurling title together in 1980.

1262 Which family won a remarkable 19 All-Ireland senior football medals between 1975 and 1986?

1263 Name the father and son who were involved in an All-Ireland football final as manager and player in the 1990s.

1264 Name the three famous Wexford brothers who left an incredible mark on hurling through their exploits in the 1950s and 1960s..

1265 Name the father and son who won All-Ireland medals for Down in the 1960s and 1990s.

1266 Two Clare brothers won All-Irelands with Clare in 1995 and 1997 but their father won a national league medal with Clare in 1977. Name the father.

1267 Name the four brothers who played in the 1987 All-Ireland senior hurling final.

1268 Name the family which had five members (another was a sub in 1993) on the Sarsfields team which won back-to-back club All-Ireland titles in 1993 and 1994.

1269 Name the two brothers who won an All-Ireland hurling title with Cork in 1986.

1270 Name the two brothers who won an All-Ireland with Limerick in 1973 and who both subsequently went on to manage Limerick.

ANSWERS PAGE 214

1271 Offaly had three sets of brothers on the team that won the 1994 All-Ireland title. Name them.

1272 Name the four Connors (brothers and cousins) who won six All-Stars between 1978 and 1983.

1273 Name the three brothers who played for Cork on Munster final day in 2003 at minor and senior level.

1274 Name the footballing family which dominated the Clann na Gael team that reached four All-Ireland club finals in a row between 1987 and 1990.

1275 Sean Og, Niall and Paudie Sheehy were the first three brothers to start and finish on a winning All-Ireland senior football team in 1962. Which county did they play for?

1276 Two families have won Ulster senior football titles in the last five years with the father as manager and son or sons as players. Name the families.

1277 Name the Kilkenny manager who coached the county to All-Ireland titles in 1979, 1982 and 1983 when his two brothers were also on those teams.

1278 Name the family with the rare distinction of winning All-Ireland senior hurling medals in three generations.

1279 Name the four brothers who played in the 1970 All-Ireland final for Wexford.

1280 Name the father and son who were on opposite sides in the 2002 football championship as manager and selector.

GENERAL KNOWLEDGE

1281 Which team halted Armagh's unbeaten run in Ulster and their quest for four Ulster titles in a row in 2007?

1282 Name the Clare goalkeeper who took over from David Fitzgerald after 18 seasons in 2007.

1283 Who captained Loughrea to the 2007 All-Ireland club hurling final?

1284 Who won the 2004 All-Ireland club hurling title?

1285 What year did Armagh win their first National Football League title?

1286 What year did Kildare last win a Leinster football title?

1287 Which two counties did Martin Carney play football for?

1288 Which county competed in the 2007 Ulster hurling championship after an absence of 61 years?

1289 How many Ulster hurling titles did Antrim win between 2002 and 2007 (inclusive)?

1290 What year did Brian Whelehan captain Offaly to an All-Ireland minor hurling title?

1291 Who did Dr Crokes beat after a replay in the 2007 All-Ireland club football semi-final?

1292 Which current Galway hurling selector won All-Ireland medals with Galway on the field of play in 1987 and 1988?

1293 Name the Sligo football manager in 2007.

1294 The current Antrim football manager, Jody Gormley, played championship football with Tyrone and which other county?

1295 Leighton Glynn is a current dual player with which county?

1296 Prior to 2007, when was the first time that Ulster failed to have a representative in the All-Ireland football semi-finals?

1297 Munster rugby player Tomas O'Leary captained Cork to an All-Ireland minor title in which year?

1298 Offaly stopped Kerry going for five All-Irelands in a row in 1982 but which county stopped Kerry's bid to achieve that feat in 1933?

1299 Name the last hurler to win All-Ireland senior medals in three different decades.

1300 Name the player who won an All-Ireland football medal with Offaly in 1982 and a Connacht senior football title with Mayo in 1985.

LEINSTER FOOTBALL FINALS

1301 How many finals did Dublin contest between 2005 and 2007?

1302 Between 2000 and 2006, how many finals went to replays?

1303 Who managed Offaly to the 1997 Leinster title?

1304 Who scored the winning point for Dublin from a '45 in the 2005 Leinster final?

1305 Who did Kildare beat in the final to win the 1998 Leinster title?

1306 When Dublin won the 2002 Leinster title, how many years had it been since their previous title?

1307 Who captained Westmeath to the 2004 Leinster title?

1308 Who captained Dublin to win the 2005 title?

1309 Which county contested six finals in a row between 1994 and 1999?

1310 Prior to 2007, when was the last time a final failed to produce a goal?

1311 How many finals did Laois contest between 2003 and 2007?

ANSWERS PAGE 214

1312 Over the last 15 years, which year did Dublin hammer Meath in the final by ten points?

1313 Name the Laois player who was top scorer in the 2005 final with 0-5.

1314 How many Leinster titles did Dublin win between 1992 and 1995 inclusive?

1315 Name the Meath player who scored the only goal of the 1999 final.

1316 Name the Kildare player who scored the only goal of the 1998 final.

1317 Who captained Offaly to the 1997 title?

1318 Name the Westmeath corner-forward who was top scorer in the 2004 final replay with 0-4 from play.

1319 Kildare trailed by six points at half-time of the 2000 Leinster final replay but which two players scored goals inside the opening two minutes of the half to draw them level?

1320 Between 1998 and 2006 inclusive, there were 14 goals scored in 11 Leinster finals (including replays) but name the player who scored three of those goals.

ANSWERS PAGE 214

HURLING GOALS GALORE

1321 Name the Kilkenny goalscorer in the 2006 All-Ireland hurling final.

1322 Name the Cork hurler who scored goals in the 2005 and 2006 All-Ireland finals.

1323 Name the Wexford hurler who scored the goal in the dying seconds of the 2004 Leinster semi-final that denied Kilkenny the opportunity to win seven Leinster titles in a row.

1324 Who were Tipperary's two goalscorers in the 1997 All-Ireland final?

1325 Who scored the only goal in the 1997 Munster hurling final between Clare and Tipperary?

1326 Who were Kilkenny's two goalscorers in the 2002 All-Ireland final?

1327 John Fenton scored one of the greatest goals of all time in the 1987 Munster championship against Limerick but who was the Limerick goalkeeper that day?

1328 Who scored Kilkenny's only goal in the 1998 All-Ireland final?

1329 Who scored the only goal in the 1996 All-Ireland final?

ANSWERS PAGE 214

1330 Name the Galway forward who scored four goals against Laois in the 2006 All-Ireland qualifiers.

1331 Who scored Waterford's only goal in the 2006 All-Ireland semi-final against Cork?

1332 Name the player who scored three goals in the 2005 All-Ireland semi-final between Galway and Kilkenny.

1333 Who scored the only goal in the 1991 All-Ireland final?

1334 Who scored Cork's only goal in the 1992 All-Ireland final?

1335 Who scored Kilkenny's goal in the dying minutes of the 1993 All-Ireland final?

1336 Who scored six goals in the 2004 Munster championship?

1337 Who scored Kilkenny's only goal in the 2003 All-Ireland final?

1338 Who scored Offaly's only goal in the 2000 All-Ireland final?

1339 There were only two goals scored in the 1987 and 1988 All-Ireland finals but the same player got both goals. Name him.

1340 In the 1983 All-Ireland semi-final, Jimmy Barry-Murphy scored one of the greatest goals of all time by doubling on John Fenton's strike. But who was the Galway goalkeeper who was beaten by that shot?

MATCH THE HURLER TO HIS COUNTY

1341 Gerry O'Grady

1342 Kevin Hartnett

1343 John Dalton

1344 Pat Mullaney

1345 Aidan Kearney

1346 Kevin Brady

1347 Gary Maguire

1348 Paul Braniff

1349 Pat Coady

1350 Darren McCormack

1351 Hugh Moloney

1352 Paul Cleary

1353 Kevin Tobin

1354 Declan Coulter

1355 Shane Brick

1356 Paudie Reidy

1357 Joe Bergin

1358 Liam Hinphey

1359 Brian Forde

1360 Fergal Moore

ANSWERS PAGE 215

FOOTBALL GOALS GALORE

1361 Who were Kerry's two goalscorers in the 2005 All-Ireland football final?

1362 Who scored the only goal in the 2002 All-Ireland final?

1363 Who scored the only goal in the 2000 replayed All-Ireland final?

1364 Which player scored two goals in the 2006 All-Ireland final?

1365 Eoin Brosnan and Kieran Donaghy scored two of Kerry's three goals in the 2006 All-Ireland quarter-final against Armagh but who scored a cracker with the third?

1366 Name the Dublin player who scored goals in the 2006 Leinster final and All-Ireland semi-final.

1367 Name the Offaly player who scored three goals against Dublin in a league game in 2006.

1368 Name the player who hit 4-5 against Galway in a league game in 2004.

1369 Name the Kerry player who scored two goals against Armagh in the 2000 All-Ireland semi-final replay.

1370 Who scored a lobbed goal over the head of Galway goalkeeper Pat Coyne in the 1983 All-Ireland senior football final for Dublin?

1371 Name the Tyrone player who scored a sensational solo goal in the 2005 drawn All-Ireland quarter-final against Dublin.

1372 Who scored Mayo's opening goal after just five minutes of the 2004 All-Ireland final?

1373 Name the defender who rescued Armagh with a late goal in the drawn 2000 All-Ireland semi-final.

1374 Who scored the only goal in the 1994 All-Ireland senior final?

1375 Shane Lennon scored more goals in the 2007 National League than anyone else. Which county does he play for?

1376 Which player became the first since Jimmy Keaveney in 1977 to find the net in both national finals (league and championship) in the same year in 2006?

1377 Name the Ulster player who scored four goals in just four championship games in 2004.

1378 Name the Tyrone forward who scored four goals in two All-Ireland U-21 finals against Kerry in 1990 and 1991.

1379 Name the Meath player who scored three goals against Westmeath in the 2001 drawn and replayed All-Ireland quarter-finals.

1380 Name the player who scored four goals for Kerry in the 1990 All-Ireland U-21 final against Tyrone.

ANSWERS PAGE 215

GREAT COMEBACKS

1381 Who were Offaly's two goalscorers in their historic late charge from five points down with five minutes remaining in the 1994 All-Ireland hurling final?

1382 Tipperary were nine points down at the three-quarter stage of the 1991 Munster final replay until goals from Pat Fox and Declan Carr pulled them back into the match. However, name the player who scored their last goal after a 'solo run', sparking pandemonium and a pitch invasion.

1383 Who was Mayo's goalscorer in their second-half surge to reel in Dublin during the 2006 All-Ireland semi-final?

1384 Which county came back from eight points down at half-time to win the 1968 All-Ireland hurling title?

1385 Who did Cork beat in the 2007 All-Ireland U-21 football final after coming from three points down with three minutes remaining?

1386 Who scored the equalising point in the drawn 1996 All-Ireland football as Meath came from six points down against Mayo?

1387 Which team did Kilkenny beat in the 1997 All-Ireland hurling quarter-final after trailing heavily at half-time?

1388 Which side did Erins Isle beat in the 1998 All-Ireland club semi-final after scoring two late goals?

ANSWERS PAGE 215

1389 Toomevara captured the 2006 Munster club hurling title after a late scoring surge against what team?

1390 Who scored the equalising goal for Meath in the final minute of the fourth game in their 1991 Leinster championship epic first-round saga?

1391 Who scored the winning point in the above match in injury time?

1392 Ahead by four points with six minutes remaining in the 1984 Munster hurling final, name the two late Cork goalscorers who denied Tipp the title.

1393 Cork trailed Galway by seven points early in the second half of the 1990 All-Ireland final but ended up winning on a scoreline of 5-15 to 2-21. Name three of Cork's goalscorers.

1394 With 20 minutes left Cork were eight points clear in the 1972 All-Ireland hurling final but which side came with a late surge to deny them the title?

1395 Kerry were ahead by two points with time almost up in the 1958 All-Ireland football semi-final when Sean O'Connell scored a goal to put which county into their first ever All-Ireland final?

1396 Limerick came from ten points down to draw the 1996 Munster hurling final but which player got the equalising point?

1397 Cork trailed Limerick by six points with ten minutes remaining in the 1956 Munster hurling final but which player scored three late goals to help Cork secure the title?

1398 Which county trailed Tipperary by 15 points in the 1956 National League hurling final but ended up winning by four?

1399 Down by seven points with 25 minutes remaining in the 1992 National Hurling League final, which player eventually scored the winning point for Limerick to secure the title?

1400 Offaly were ahead by 11 points shortly after half-time in the 1970 Leinster football final but which side made a sensational comeback to win one of the greatest ever Leinster finals by a point?

ANSWERS PAGE 215

MATCH THE FOOTBALLER TO HIS COUNTY

1401   David Barden

1402   Paddy Keenan

1403   Conor Whelan

1404   Pa Ranahan

1405   Gary Connaughton

1406   Thomas Deehan

1407   Alan Quirke

1408   Michael McNamara

1409   Kevin Brady

1410   Ronan Sweeney

1411   James Reilly

1412   Mark Lynch

1413   John Tiernan

1414   Ciaran Deely

1415   Dick Clerkin

1416   Mark Little

1417   Ciaran Duignan

1418   Neville Coughlan

1419   Malachy Mackin

1420   Daniel Hughes

ANSWERS PAGE 215

FOOTBALL PENALTIES SCORED AND MISSED

1421 Who scored Meath's penalty goal in the 1996 replayed All-Ireland football final?

1422 Who scored Kildare's goal from a penalty in the 2003 Leinster final against Laois?

1423 Name the Mayo player who scored their only goal from a penalty in the 1997 All-Ireland final.

1424 Name the Dublin player who hit a late penalty off the crossbar in their narrow defeat to Meath in the 1997 Leinster football quarter-final.

1425 Name the goalkeeper who saved Oisin McConville's penalty in the 2002 All-Ireland football final.

1426 Name the goalkeeper who saved Mikey Sheehy's penalty in the famous 1982 All-Ireland football final.

1427 The first penalty in an All-Ireland final came in 1948, which Padraig Carney scored for which county?

1428 Name the Kerry player who scored twice from the penalty spot in the 2000 Munster semi-final against Cork.

1429 Name the Cork goalkeeper who saved a penalty in the 1999 All-Ireland final.

1430 Name the Mayo player who scored a penalty against Galway in the 1996 Connacht final.

1431 Name the Cork player who scored two goals from the penalty spot in the 1989 All-Ireland semi-final against Dublin.

1432 Liam Sammon had a chance to put Galway four points up 12 minutes into the second half of the 1974 All-Ireland final but his shot was brilliantly saved by which keeper?

1433 Name the Tyrone player who coolly slotted a penalty against Galway in the second half of the 1986 All-Ireland final.

1434 Name the Dublin player who missed a penalty against Donegal in the 1992 All-Ireland final.

1435 The famous Dublin-Meath four-game saga in 1991 would probably never have happened if which Meath player hadn't held his nerve and slotted home a vital penalty in the first game?

1436 Name the Dublin player who drove a penalty wide late in the third replay of the Dublin-Meath saga in 1991.

1437 Kildare were down to 13 men at the time and had no regular penalty taker but which player scored a crucial penalty to give them victory against Laois in the 1997 Leinster quarter-final?

1438 Dublin needed a goal from the penalty spot in the last minute of the 1988 Leinster final against Meath but which player drove the ball over the bar?

1439 Name the Down goalkeeper who saved Charlie Redmond's penalty in the 1994 All-Ireland final.

1440 Name the Armagh player who missed a penalty against Kerry in the 1953 All-Ireland final.

CONTROVERSIAL SCORES THAT WERE AND WEREN'T REGISTERED

1441 Which Offaly hurler scored a controversial handpassed goal in the closing stages of the 1981 All-Ireland final?

1442 In the 2007 Leinster football quarter-final, which county had an apparently legal goal disallowed against Laois for a square ball at a critical stage of the game?

1443 The winning goal in the 1982 All-Ireland final was laced with controversy because the goalscorer was thought by many to have pushed which Kerry player before he caught the ball?

1444 In their Munster football championship tie with Tipperary in 1999, a shot from a Kerry forward cannoned off the back stanchion of the goal and rebounded from where he netted. The ball had gone wide but the umpire signalled the goal for which player?

1445 Tipperary claimed they had a point waved wide in the first half of the 1997 All-Ireland final. Name the player who took that shot.

1446 Westmeath scored a point in the first round of the 2004 Leinster championship against Offaly that was subsequently shown to be wide. Westmeath went on to win the Leinster title but which player scored that point?

1447 In the 2007 Ulster championship quarter-final, Armagh goalkeeper Paul Hearty dropped a ball into the net in the dying minutes but Donegal's Kevin Cassidy was clearly in the square when the ball dropped. Name the goalscorer.

1448 Trailing by a point with time almost up in the 1995 All-Ireland football final, Peter Canavan set up a fellow Tyrone player for the equalising score but the referee subsequently blew for a free out. Who was the Tyrone player who scored that point that never was?

1449 Name the Limerick hurler who scored the winning point from a '65 with the last puck of the 1973 Munster hurling final which looked to have veered wide at the last second.

1450 In the 1985 All-Ireland hurling final – which Offaly won by two points – a long ball from Galway's Joe Cooney appeared to have dropped over the Offaly goal-line. Which goalkeeper scooped the ball to safety?

1451 In the 1982 Leinster hurling semi-final, Offaly had a goal scored against Laois which passed outside the post and under the net to earn Offaly a draw. Name the player credited with that goal.

1452 In the 1982 Leinster hurling final, name the Offaly goalkeeper who thought the ball had gone wide before Liam Fennelly swept it across the square for Matt Ruth to finish to the net.

ANSWERS PAGE 216

1453 In the last ten years, Raymond Cunningham scored a point in a provincial final for his team which TV pictures later showed was wide. That team won by a point but name the team and the final.

1454 In the drawn 2007 Leinster quarter-final between Dublin and Meath, who scored Dublin's only goal, which appeared to be a blatant square ball?

1455 In the 1976 Munster football final replay with Kerry trailing, a late Sean Walsh shot that squeezed past Billy Morgan was stopped on the line by Brian Murphy. However, Murphy staggered and which famous Munster referee allowed the goal to stand?

1456 In the dying moments of the drawn 1991 Munster hurling final, Tipperary were trailing by a point when which player had a kicked shot for a point controversially waved wide?

1457 In the 1953 Munster hurling final between Cork and Tipperary, a ball from Mossie O'Riordan was sent to the net by Liam Dowling. However the referee had already blown for a foul on O'Riordan, but a quiet word from a player (from the team which had scored the goal) seemed to alter the decision. The team that won the game went on to win that year's All-Ireland. Name that team.

1458 In scoring his first and favourite championship goal, DJ Carey took approximately 12 steps before kicking the ball to the net to edge out Wexford in the 1991 Leinster semi-final. Name the Wexford goalkeeper that day.

1459 Mayo led in the dying moments of the 1946 Connacht football final, but a shot from a Roscommon player, according to the Mayo players, went wide and bounced off the umpire's legs. Which Roscommon player famously ran in, kicked the ball to the net and waved the green flag himself? (A replay was later ordered which Roscommon won.)

1460 In the 1989 Connacht minor football final, Roscommon won a late penalty but as the designated penalty taker was about to take it, another player arrived out of nowhere and blasted the ball to the net. Roscommon won the match but were subsequently later ordered to replay the match, which they won. Name the penalty scorer who caused all the controversy.

ANSWERS PAGE 216

CLUB CALL 3

Match the county to the following clubs

1461 Glenariffe

1462 Kilmaley

1463 Bride Rovers

1464 Stabannon Parnells

1465 Killererin

1466 Killyclogher

1467 Clontibret

1468 Kilcar

1469 Roanmore

1470 Dunnamaggin

1471 Faythe Harriers

1472 Coolderry

1473 Bonnyconnellan

1474 Skryne

1475 Ballybrown

1476 St Sylvesters

1477 Loughmore-Castleiney

1478 Kerins O'Rahillys

1479 Slaughtneil

1480 Lixnaw

ANSWERS PAGE 216

NAME THE YEAR 2

1481 Anthony Cunningham captains Galway to an All-Ireland U-21 hurling title, a week after he and a host of his teammates had lost an All-Ireland senior final.

1482 O'Hanrahans win the Leinster club football title.

1483 The fingertips of Anthony Tohill deny Shenny McQuillan a late point and the chance for Antrim to reach an Ulster senior final.

1484 Crossmaglen Rangers win their first Ulster club football title.

1485 Tom Hickey captains Kilkenny in an All-Ireland hurling final.

1486 Dessie Dolan misses a 20-metre free and the opportunity to give Westmeath their first victory over Meath in the championship.

1487 Galway reach their fourth All-Ireland hurling final in a row in the 1980s.

1488 DJ Carey wins his first All-Star award.

1489 Thomond College, Limerick win the All-Ireland club football title.

1490 Pat Cleary scores two goals in an All-Ireland hurling final for Offaly.

ANSWERS PAGE 216

1491 Former Kerry great John O'Keeffe manages Clare to a Munster football final.

1492 DJ Carey scores 3-3 out of 3-5 in an All-Ireland Colleges final for St Kieran's against St Flannan's.

1493 Eamonn Coleman manages Derry to his second All-Ireland semi-final.

1494 Paidi O Se leads Kerry to their first Munster senior title under his management.

1495 Ciaran Carey captains Limerick in an All-Ireland senior hurling final.

1496 Nemo Rangers lose an All-Ireland club final to Crossmolina.

1497 Timmy Houlihan captains Limerick to an All-Ireland U-21 hurling title.

1498 James 'Cha' Fitzpatrick captains Kilkenny to an All-Ireland U-21 hurling title.

1499 Tyrone win their first National Football League title.

1500 Donegal contest their first Nicky Rackard Cup final.

MINOR MATTERS – THE LAST 15 YEARS

1501 What year did Laois win their first All-Ireland minor football title?

1502 What year did Galway's Joe Canning attempt to win his third All-Ireland minor hurling medal in a row?

1503 What year did Paul Flynn play in an All-Ireland minor hurling final for Waterford?

1504 Which year did Dublin win the Leinster minor title but were beaten in the All-Ireland final by the same team they'd already beaten in the Leinster final?

1505 What year did Laois' Brian 'Beano' McDonald attempt to win his third All-Ireland minor football medal in a row?

1506 Who were the first back-door winners of the All-Ireland minor football title?

1507 What year did Sean Og O hAilpin, Donal Og Cusack, Timmy McCarthy and Joe Deane win All-Ireland minor medals together with Cork?

1508 Who were the second team to win an All-Ireland minor football title through the 'back door'?

1509 Between 2001 and 2006 (inclusive) how many All-Ireland minor football finals went to replays?

1510 What year did Benny Coulter, Ronan Murtagh, Liam Doyle and Michael Walsh win an All-Ireland minor football title with Down?

1511 What year did Ronan Curran and Niall McCarthy win All-Ireland minor medals with Cork?

1512 Tyrone's Sean Cavanagh won an All-Ireland minor title in what year?

1513 Mark Vaughan lined out in an All-Ireland minor football final for Dublin in what year?

1514 Mayo contested three All-Ireland minor football finals between 1999 and 2005 but how many did they win?

1515 What year did Clare win their first All-Ireland minor hurling title?

1516 Jimmy Barry Murphy coached Cork to how many All-Ireland minor hurling finals?

1517 What year did Declan Browne win an All-Ireland minor hurling medal with Tipperary?

1518 Galway's Kevin Broderick played as a goalkeeper in an All-Ireland minor final in what year?

1519 In 1994 Galway won an All-Ireland minor hurling title and it was the first time that a Galway team had defeated that particular county in an All-Ireland hurling final. Name the county.

1520 The Cork player who captained an All-Ireland minor winning side in 1998 was the son of a former Cork All-Ireland senior winning captain. Name either the father or the son.

ANSWERS PAGE 216

HURLING SCORES FROM PLACED BALLS

1521 Who scored Clare's last point of the 1995 All-Ireland final from a free?

1522 Who scored Cork's opening goal in the 1986 All-Ireland final from a close-in free?

1523 Prior to 2007, name the only player to score goals from frees in three Munster finals over the last 15 years.

1524 Name the Kilkenny player who scored a goal from a penalty in the 1992 All-Ireland final.

1525 Name the Clare midfielder who scored a first-half point from a sideline cut in the 1995 All-Ireland final.

1526 Name the Offaly player who scored a goal from a 20-metre free in the 1994 All-Ireland final.

1527 Name the Clare player who scored a goal from a penalty in the 1995 Munster final.

1528 Who scored Cork's goal from a long-range free in the 2004 Munster semi-final against Limerick?

1529 Name the Kilkenny forward who blasted a 20-metre free to the net against Galway in the 2004 All-Ireland quarter-final.

1530 Who scored a goal for Wexford from a penalty against Offaly in the 1996 Leinster final?

1531 Name the Clare defender who scored seven points from placed balls in the 1999 drawn All-Ireland quarter-final against Galway.

1532 Name the Limerick player who scored a '65 with the last puck of the game in extra-time of the 2007 replayed Munster semi-final against Tipperary.

1533 Name the Kilkenny player who scored a goal from a sideline cut in the opening seconds of the 1999 Leinster semi-final against Laois.

1534 Who scored Clare's equalising point with the last puck of the game in the 1998 drawn All-Ireland semi-final against Offaly?

1535 Name the young Ballygunner clubman who scored the winning point for De La Salle from a long-range free in the dying minutes of the 2007 All-Ireland colleges final.

1536 Name the Cork player who scored two points from sideline cuts in the 1992 Munster final.

1537 Name the Wexford player who scored two goals from a penalty and a close-in free against Limerick in the 2001 All-Ireland quarter-final.

1538 Who scored Tipperary's equalising point from a free against Cork in the drawn 1987 Munster final?

1539 Who scored Clare's only goal against Galway in the 2002 All-Ireland quarter-final from a snap free while Jamesie O'Connor was getting ready to strike the ball?

1540 Name the Wexford forward who scored three points from sideline cuts in the 1993 drawn Leinster final.

UNDER-21 QUESTIONS FROM THE LAST 15 YEARS

1541 What year did Brendan Cummins and Tommy Dunne win All-Ireland U-21 medals with Tipperary?

1542 How many All-Ireland U-21 medals did Donal Og Cusack, Sean Og O'hAilpin, Joe Deane and Timmy McCarthy win with Cork?

1543 What two years were the All-Ireland U-21 hurling and football finals staged as a double-header in Semple Stadium, Thurles?

1544 Galway contested five All-Ireland U-21 hurling finals in a row between 1996 and 2000 but how many did they win?

1545 What year did Limerick reach All-Ireland U-21 football and hurling finals in the same season?

1546 Tyrone contested six All-Ireland U-21 finals between 1990 and 2003 but how many did they win?

1547 What year did goalkeeper Diarmuid Murphy captain Kerry to an All-Ireland U-21 football title?

1548 What year did Armagh win their first All-Ireland U-21 football title?

1549 Who captained Westmeath to their first and only All-Ireland U-21 football title?

1550 Trevor Giles won an All-Ireland U-21 football title a week before he played in an All-Ireland minor football final. Name the year.

ANSWERS PAGE 217

1551 What year did Joe Bergin captain Galway to an All-Ireland U-21 football title?

1552 Who captained Kilkenny to the 2006 All-Ireland hurling title?

1553 How many Leinster U-21 hurling finals did Dublin contest between 2002 and 2007?

1554 Jackie Tyrrell captained Kilkenny to an All-Ireland U-21 hurling title in what year?

1555 Name the Galway hurler who played in four All-Ireland U-21 hurling finals in a row between 1996 and 1999?

1556 What year did Declan Ruth, Rory McCarthy and Paul Codd play in an All-Ireland U-21 hurling final for Wexford?

1557 What year did Philly Larkin captain Kilkenny to an All-Ireland U-21 hurling title?

1558 Kerry won seven Munster U-21 football titles between 1992 and 1999 and contested five All-Ireland finals in that timespan. How many finals did they win?

1559 When did Cavan last contest an All-Ireland U-21 football final?

1560 Only four players have managed to win All-Ireland U-21 hurling and football medals on the field of play in the same year but one managed it in the last ten years. Name him.

FOOTBALLERS AND THEIR CLUBS 2

Match the player to his club

1561 Kieran Fitzgerald (Galway)

1562 Kieran McGeeney (Armagh)

1563 Brendan Devenny (Donegal)

1564 Mark Stanfield (Louth)

1565 Aidan O'Mahony (Kerry)

1566 Sean Cavanagh (Tyrone)

1567 Ciaran McDonald (Mayo)

1568 Michael Donnellan (Galway)

1569 Ryan McMenamin (Tyrone)

1570 Andy Mallon (Armagh)

1571 Joe Bergin (Galway)

1572 Graham Geraghty (Meath)

1573 Conal Keaney (Dublin)

1574 Enda Muldoon (Derry)

1575 Anthony Lynch (Cork)

1576 Colm McFadden (Donegal)

1577 Ronan Sweeney (Kildare)

1578 Ciaran McManus (Offaly)

1579 Brendan Quigley (Laois)

1580 Tom O'Sullivan (Kerry)

NAME THE MISSING LINK IN THE LINE OR THE PARTNERSHIP

1581 ?, Brian Stafford, Bernard Flynn

1582 Peter Finnerty, Tony Keady, ?

1583 Liam Doyle, ? , Anthony Daly

1584 Derek Savage, ? , Neil Finnegan

1585 ?, Kieran Donaghy, Mike Frank Russell

1586 ?, Eoin Liston, John Egan

1587 Mark O'Reilly, ? ,Cormac Murphy

1588 Brian McGilligan and ?

1589 Enda Colleran, ?, J B McDermott

1590 Gay O'Driscoll, ? , Robbie Kelleher

1591 Liam Hayes and ?

1592 Sylvie Linnane, ? , Ollie Kilkenny

1593 Brian Whelehan, Hubert Rigney, ?

1594 Rod Guiney, ? , Larry O'Gorman

1595 John Gardiner, Ronan Curran, ?

1596 Charlie McCarthy, ? , Seanie O'Leary

1597 Pat Fox, Cormac Bonnar, ?

1598 Michael O'Halloran, Brian Lohan, ?

1599 Dermot McCurtain, ? , Denis Coughlan

1600 ? , Michael Maher, Kieran Carey

CRUCIAL AND OUTSTANDING FOOTBALL SCORES FROM PLACED BALLS

1601 Who scored the equalising point from a sideline ball in the dying seconds of the 2001 All-Ireland quarter-final between Kerry and Dublin?

1602 Name the Westmeath forward who kicked the winning point in extra-time from a sideline ball in the 2001 fourth-round qualifier against Mayo.

1603 Trailing heavily in the 2003 drawn Ulster football final, which player scored Tyrone's only goal from a second-half penalty to haul them back into the match?

1604 Who scored an outstanding point from a sideline ball in the 1998 All-Ireland final for Galway

1605 Name the Meath player who equalised from a sideline ball in injury time of the 2007 drawn Leinster quarter-final against Dublin.

1606 Who scored the equalising point for Dublin from a free in injury time of the 2005 drawn All-Ireland quarter-final against Tyrone?

1607 Who scored the winning point from a free for Tyrone in the 2005 All-Ireland semi-final?

1608 Who scored the equalising point for Galway in the dying minutes of the 1998 drawn Connacht football final?

1609 Who scored the winning point for Tyrone in the 2007 Ulster quarter-final against Fermanagh from a long-range free?

1610 Who scored the equalising point from a '45 with the last kick of the game in the drawn 2003 Leinster quarter-final between Offaly and Laois?

1611 Who scored the equalising point for Cork from a free with the last kick of the game in the 1987 drawn Munster final against Kerry?

1612 Who scored the equalising point for Tyrone in the dying seconds of the 2003 Ulster quarter-final against Derry?

1613 Name the Fermanagh player who scored a point with a sideline ball to take the 2004 Round 3 qualifier against Meath to extra-time.

1614 Name the Offaly player who scored the winning point from a sideline ball in the dying minutes of the 2002 Leinster quarter-final against Laois.

1615 Who was the referee who gave the controversial free that resulted in Kerry's Mikey Sheehy chipping Dublin goalkeeper Paddy Cullen for a crucial goal in the 1978 All-Ireland football final?

1616 Name the goalkeeper who scored 1-1 from placed balls in a football championship game that went to a replay in 2004.

1617 Who scored the equalising point for Kerry from a free in the drawn 2000 All-Ireland semi-final against Armagh?

ANSWERS PAGE 217

1618 Who scored the equalising point for Meath against Cork in the drawn 1988 All-Ireland final?

1619 Who scored the equalising point for Cork from a placed ball in the dying seconds of the drawn 1987 All-Ireland semi-final against Galway

1620 Name the Monaghan player who scored a monstrous equalising free from 55 yards against Kerry in the drawn 1985 All-Ireland football semi-final.

GENERAL KNOWLEDGE

1621 What years did Galway win their famous three All-Ireland football titles in a row?

1622 Who captained Mayo in the 2004 All-Ireland football final?

1623 What year did Ger Cunningham retire from inter-county hurling after 18 years as Cork's first-choice goalkeeper?

1624 When did Down last win an Ulster senior hurling title?

1625 Who managed Nemo Rangers to the 2003 All-Ireland club football title?

1626 Who managed Sligo to the 2002 All-Ireland football quarter-final?

1627 Which inter-county football manager in 2007 had a brother on the team he was managing?

1628 The former Armagh footballer Des Mackin played in an All-Ireland club final in the last ten years with which club?

1629 What club does Damien Fitzhenry play for in Wexford?

1630 Who captained Galway in the 2000 All-Ireland football final?

1631 Who scored the only goal in the 1989 All-Ireland football final?

1632 Who scored the only goal in the 1995 All-Ireland football final?

1633 Who won the Tommy Murphy Cup in 2006?

1634 Who captained Galway in the 2001 All-Ireland hurling final?

1635 Name the only player to play in All-Ireland club hurling and football finals over the last 15 years.

1636 Name the three brothers who played on the Antrim team that won the 2007 Ulster hurling title.

1637 Who captained Tipperary to the 2006 All-Ireland minor title?

1638 Which current Offaly hurler is the son of a late great Offaly player who won an All-Ireland in 1981?

1639 Name the only player to captain his county in four All-Ireland senior finals over the last 35 years.

1640 Two players have twice missed penalties in All-Ireland finals over the last 15 years. Name them.

LEGENDS OF HURLING AND FOOTBALL

1641 What club did Offaly's Matt Connor play for?

1642 How many Railway Cup medals did Christy Ring win with Munster?

1643 What club did Nicky Rackard play for in Wexford?

1644 How many All-Ireland medals did Mick O'Connell win with Kerry?

1645 How many All-Ireland senior titles did Kevin Heffernan win with Dublin as a player?

1646 What club did Lory Meagher play for in Kilkenny?

1647 How many All-Ireland senior titles did Mick Mackey win with Limerick?

1648 What year did Eddie Keher captain Kilkenny to an All-Ireland title?

1649 Sean Purcell played for which club in Galway?

1650 How many All-Star awards did Brian Whelehan win?

1651 Mick O'Dwyer won how many All-Ireland senior titles with Kerry as a player?

1652 Name Seamus Moynihan's club.

ANSWERS PAGE 218

1653 Name the two clubs Jack O'Shea played for during his career.

1654 How many All-Ireland senior medals did Jimmy Doyle win with Tipperary?

1655 How many county titles did DJ Carey win with Young Irelands?

1656 What club did John Doyle play for in Tipperary?

1657 How many Ulster club titles did Peter Canavan win?

1658 What club did Down's Sean O'Neill play for?

1659 What year was Mikey Sheehy selected as Footballer of the Year?

1660 John Joe O'Reilly won how many All-Ireland senior football titles with Cavan?

MUNSTER'S FINEST HURLERS – WHO AM I?

1661 Although he suffered the disappointment of captaining Tipperary to two All-Ireland hurling final defeats in 1967 and 1968, this player was regarded as one of the finest centre-backs of all time.

1662 He was from the Na Piarsaigh club in Cork, who won three All-Ireland senior medals between 1984 and 1990, and he was also a Cork footballer.

1663 He won an All-Ireland senior medal with Limerick in 1973 but he was also a highly accomplished shot putter who represented Ireland on four occasions. Sadly his career was cut short in 1979 after suffering a serious eye injury.

1664 He won an All-Ireland senior medal as a player in 1973 and an All-Ireland title as a manager in the 1990s.

1665 He won two All-Ireland hurling medals with Limerick but his son won eight All-Ireland football medals with Kerry.

1666 He captained Clare to National League success in 1978 and was selected at centre-back in 1984 on the greatest team to have never won an All-Ireland.

1667 He was born in Offaly, with whom he played minor hurling, but he played in three All-Ireland senior finals for Limerick, winning an All-Ireland in 1973.

ANSWERS PAGE 218

1668 He won five All-Ireland senior medals but he captained Cork to the All-Ireland senior title in 1966 when he was still only 21.

1669 He won an All-Ireland club medal with Midleton in 1988 and was chosen as an All-Star for five consecutive seasons between 1983 and 1987.

1670 He scored one of the greatest points of all time when landing the winning score against Clare in the 1996 Munster semi-final.

1671 He played for Clare between 1993 and 2006, winning All-Irelands in 1995 and 1997 as well as four All-Stars. Voted Player of the Fitzgibbon Tournament in 1994, he also captained his club to an All-Ireland club final in 1997.

1672 He played as a defender in the 1985 Munster final but he made his name as a corner-forward and was named Hurler of the Year in 1991.

1673 He won four All-Star awards between 1991 and 1996 and captained his county in the 1994 All-Ireland final.

1674 He won three All-Stars as a centre-back as well as an All-Ireland club hurling medal with St Joseph's Doora-Barefield.

1675 He won four All-Irelands with Tipperary in the 1960s and was chosen as Hurler of the Year in 1962.

1676 A brilliant midfielder who captained Waterford to a Munster title in 1957, he also won 12 county championship medals with Mount Sion, including nine in a row.

1677 He captained Cork to their three-in-a-row of All-Ireland titles in 1978 and is amongst the top ten championship hurling scorers of all time.

1678 He won All-Ireland medals with Tipperary in 1989 and 1991 and was a Tipperary hurling selector in 2006 and 2007.

1679 He won four All-Ireland medals with Cork, scored the opening goal in the Centenary All-Ireland final in 1984, was a selector on Cork's All-Ireland winning team of 1999 and is the father of a current Munster rugby player.

1680 He was from Ballyduff in Waterford and won an All-Ireland in 1959 as well as three Munster titles in 1957, 1959 and 1963.

ANSWERS PAGE 218

ODD ONE OUT

1681   Fergal Byron, Gary Connaughton, James McGarry

1682   Mayobridge, Lavey, Bryansford

1683   Donal Og Cusack, Diarmuid O'Sullivan, Ronan Curran

1684   Andy Merrigan Cup, Irish Press Cup, Tommy Moore Cup

1685   Birr, Athenry, Toomevara

1686   Nemo Rangers, Castlehaven, St Finbarr's

1687   Jack Boothman, Paddy Buggy, Nicky Brennan

1688   Seamus Moynihan, Darragh O Se, Declan O'Sullivan

1689   Camross, Castletown, Kilmessan

1690   Billy Morgan, Tony Davis, Larry Tompkins

1691   Hogan Stand, Nally Stand, Cusack Stand

1692   Willie O'Connor, Andy Comerford, Martin Comerford

1693   Pearse Stadium, Fitzgerald Stadium, Semple Stadium

1694   Dunloy, Portaferry, Cushendall

1695   Mount Sion, De La Salle, Ballygunner

1696   Na Fianna, St Vincent's, Kilmacud Crokes

1697   Gary Kirby, Mike Houlihan, Ciaran Carey

1698   Crossmolina Deel Rovers, Knockmore, Ballina Stephenites

1699   Athenry, Birr, Ballyhale Shamrocks

1700   Pat Mullaney, Stuart Reynolds, Colm Callanan

ANSWERS PAGE 218

GENERAL KNOWLEDGE

1701 Whose famous letter to Michael Cusack, written in 1884, appears in the Official Guide of the GAA to the present day?

1702 What was the first major final in which sponsors' names were allowed to appear on team playing-gear?

1703 Who scored Galway's only goal in the 2001 All-Ireland football semi-final against Derry?

1704 What is the minimum length and width (in metres) of a GAA field?

1705 Prior to the 2007 Munster hurling final, name the player who had scored goals in six successive Munster championship games.

1706 Name the former All-Ireland winning minor player with Down who is currently playing Australian Rules football.

1707 Colm Begley is currently playing Australian Rules football but which county did he win an All-Ireland minor medal with?

1708 Christy Ring holds the record number of championship appearances in hurling. How many appearances did he make?

1709 Name the two brothers who scored goals in a provincial senior football final in 2007.

1710 What was unique about the pairing of St Flannan's and Dublin Colleges in the 2006 All-Ireland Colleges hurling final?

1711 What was the name of the now defunct Connacht hurling championship trophy?

1712 Mark Bergin hit a free off the post with the last puck of the game (it would have been the equaliser) for which college in the 2007 All-Ireland Colleges final?

1713 Name the two players who played in an All-Ireland senior hurling final and a Christy Ring Cup final.

1714 In which Ulster town is the club called the Russell Gaelic Union?

1715 Name the Galway panellist for the 2005 All-Ireland hurling final who won county senior hurling medals with Portumna and UCD that year.

1716 The University College Galway team that won the Fitzgibbon Cup in 1977 contained a future All-Ireland SHC winning manager, a future president of the GAA, and two future All-Ireland SHC winning captains. Name them.

1717 Which inter-county team features an apple on its crest?

1718 What is the proper name of the GAA stadium in Tuam?

1719 In which GAA sport is the Charles Haughey Cup a prize?

1720 Prior to 2007 only 25 hurlers had hit more than 100 points (white flags) and none of those had been defenders for their entire career. Name the career defender who hit 97 points before he retired in the last five years.

MUNSTER FOOTBALL FINALS

1721 What year did Tipperary last reach a Munster final?

1722 Who was the Cork goalkeeper in the 2007 Munster final?

1723 What year did Clare last contest a Munster final?

1724 Tipperary reached successive Munster finals in 1993 and 1994 but which county defeated them on both occasions?

1725 How many Munster titles did Cork win between 1987 and 1995 inclusive?

1726 Limerick reached successive Munster football finals in 2003 and 2004 but when was their previous Munster final appearance?

1727 How many Munster finals did Tipperary contest in the 1990s?

1728 Who managed Limerick to successive Munster finals in 2003 and 2004?

1729 Who captained Clare to the 1992 Munster title?

1730 Name the Limerick player who played in three Munster finals (excluding replays) in the last 20 years.

1731 Who captained Kerry to the 2003 Munster title?

1732 Who captained Kerry in three Munster finals in a row between 2005 and 2007?

1733 Prior to 2007, when was the last time Kerry beat Cork in a Munster final in Killarney?

1734 Who was Kerry's goalscorer in the 2007 Munster final?

1735 How many Munster football titles have Waterford won?

1736 Cork beat Kerry in the 1990 Munster final by five, ten or fifteen points?

1737 Seamus Moynihan made his championship debut as an 18-year old in which year's Munster final?

1738 Who was Cork's goalscorer in the 2007 Munster final?

1739 Name the Limerick player who had three late chances from placed balls to win the 2004 drawn Munster final.

1740 Who were Clare's two goalscorers in the 1992 Munster football final?

HURLING GOALKEEPERS

1741   Which club does Kilkenny's PJ Ryan play for?

1742   How many All-Stars has Davy Fitzgerald won?

1743   Who was the Galway goalkeeper in the 2001 All-Ireland final?

1744   Who was the Kilkenny goalkeeper in the 1998 All-Ireland final?

1745   What club does Brendan Cummins play for?

1746   How many All-Ireland club hurling medals has Brian Mullins won with Birr?

1747   Name the goalkeeper who won Young Hurler of the Year in 1998.

1748   What club does Down goalkeeper Graham Clarke play for?

1749   Tadgh Flynn was UL's Fitzgibbon Cup goalkeeper for three seasons between 2005 and 2007 but which county does he play for?

1750   Dublin goalkeeper Gary Maguire plays for which club?

1751   Prior to the 2007 championship season, only five goalkeepers had managed to keep clean sheets in two All-Ireland finals. Tom Mulcahy and Dave Creedon (Cork) and John Commins (Galway) were three, but the fourth is still playing. Name him.

ANSWERS PAGE 220

1752 The current Limerick hurling goalkeeper Brian Murray is a son of which former well-known referee?

1753 Name the Waterford goalkeeper who played in the 2004 All-Ireland semi-final against Kilkenny.

1754 Ryan McGarry played in the Liam McCarthy Cup for what county in 2007?

1755 Who played in goal for Galway in the 1985 All-Ireland senior final?

1756 In the last 25 years, two goalkeepers have been selected as Texaco Hurler of the Year. Name them.

1757 Who was the last goalkeeper to play championship hurling for Wexford before Damien Fitzhenry?

1758 Name the goalkeeper who played Interprovincial hurling for Munster in 2006 even though he had still to make his inter-county championship debut.

1759 Name the only goalkeeper to score a goal from a free in an All-Ireland hurling final.

1760 Prior to 2007, only one goalkeeper in history had managed to keep three clean sheets in All-Ireland finals. Name him.

NATIONAL FOOTBALL LEAGUE FINALS

1761 How many National League finals did Donegal contest in the 1990s?

1762 Who captained Armagh to their first League title in 2005?

1763 When did Derry last win a League title?

1764 Gerard Courell is the only player to captain his county to three National League titles in a row. Which county did he play for?

1765 The highest individual score ever recorded in a National League final was a 0-12 haul by Tony McTague in the 1973 decider against Kerry. Who did McTague play for?

1766 Donegal's last three scores in the 2007 National League final came from three substitutes. Name two of them.

1767 Although he didn't start the 2007 National League final, who captained Mayo in that game?

1768 How many National League titles did Derry win between 1992 and 2000?

1769 Paddy Moclair captained Mayo to consecutive National League titles in 1937 and 1938 but only one player has managed that feat since. Name the player who has achieved that distinction in the last ten years.

1770 The 2007 National League final failed to produce a goal but when was the last league final that failed to produce a goal?

1771 Name the Armagh player who scored 0-10 in the 2005 National League final.

1772 When did Dublin last win a National League title?

1773 What year did Mike Hassett captain Kerry to a League title?

1774 When did Cork last win a League title?

1775 Name the Derry midfielder who was top scorer in the 1992 and 1996 National League finals.

1776 What year did Offaly win their only National League title (excluding the 2004 Division 2 title)?

1777 Mike Frank Russell is the joint-fifth highest individual scorer in National League finals. What year, though, did he score 1-6 in a League decider?

1778 What year did Henry Downey captain Derry to a League title?

1779 What year did Monaghan win their only League title (excluding the 2005 Division Two title)?

1780 Name the only county to win six National Leagues in a row.

FOOTBALL GOALKEEPERS

1781 Who was the Tyrone goalkeeper in the 2003 All-Ireland final?

1782 Prior to 2007, who was the last goalkeeper to save a penalty in an All-Ireland final?

1783 Mickey McQuillan played in All-Ireland finals for Meath in 1987, 1988 and 1991 but who was the Meath goalkeeper for the 1990 final?

1784 Name the goalkeeper who won an All-Ireland senior, an All-Ireland club and an All-Star award in 1998.

1785 Name the goalkeeper who won an Ulster title with Cavan in 1997 and who has since established himself as the top goalkeeping coach in the country.

1786 Name the Cork goalkeeper who played in Munster U-21 hurling and football finals in 2007.

1787 Name the Monaghan goalkeeper who won an All-Star in 1988.

1788 Goalkeeper Damien Sheridan captained what county to the last 12 of the 2006 football championship?

1789 Name the Clare goalkeeper for their three Munster final appearances in 1992, 1997 and 2000.

1790 Benny Tierney was Armagh's All-Ireland winning goalkeeper in 2002 but name the goalkeeper who played three championship matches for Armagh in 2001.

1791 Donegal goalkeeper Paul Durcan won two Sigerson Cup medals with which college?

1792 The oldest player in the football championship in 2007 was a goalkeeper. Name him.

1793 Name the only goalkeeper to have won five All-Stars.

1794 Only two goalkeepers have won the Texaco Footballer of the Year award. Name them.

1795 Name the goalkeeper who won four All-Stars between 1974 and 1979.

1796 Who was the Tyrone goalkeeper in the 1986 All-Ireland final?

1797 Name the Dublin goalkeeper who was sub to John O'Leary for a large part of the 1990s and who won an All-Ireland club medal with Kilmacud Crokes in 1995.

1798 Name the player who played as goalkeeper for Westmeath in 1996 but who was nominated for an All-Star at full-back in 2001.

1799 Who was the Galway goalkeeper for their opening two games of the 2001 Connacht championship?

1800 Only two players have won All-Irelands as a goalkeeper and an outfield player. Name them.

FOOTBALL ALL-STARS

1801 What footballer holds the record number of All-Stars?

1802 Name the two Donegal brothers who won All-Stars in 1992.

1803 Name the goalkeeper on the 2003 All-Star football team.

1804 Name the two Westmeath footballers selected on the 2004 All-Star team.

1805 Between 1978 and 1982, three sets of Offaly brothers won All-Stars. Name the three sets.

1806 Prior to 2007, who was Roscommon's only All-Star over the last 15 years?

1807 What year did Down win their highest ever total of All-Star awards with seven?

1808 Who was the 1000th All-Star?

1809 Name the Mayo brothers who won All-Stars between 1996 and 2006.

1810 Name the two Meath players with the most All-Stars (four).

1811 What year did Meath win their highest ever total of All-Stars with seven?

1812 Who won Fermanagh's two All-Stars in 2004?

ANSWERS PAGE 221

1813 Which player outside of Kerry holds the record number of All-Star awards with six?

1814 Ollie Crinnigan was the All-Star goalkeeper in 1978. What county was he from?

1815 Anthony McGurk won an All-Star in 1973 at left-full forward and an All-Star in 1975 at centre-back. What county did he play for?

1816 Name the Meath footballer who won an All-Star in 1999, 28 years after his father had won an All-Star with the same county.

1817 Name the only two Derry players to have won four All-Stars.

1818 Name the only Kerry player to win All-Stars as a defender and a forward.

1819 Name the only father and son to win All-Stars with different counties in the same province.

1820 In the last 15 years, which county won All-Stars from numbers 4 to 9 in one season?

ANSWERS PAGE 221

ALL-IRELAND HURLING SEMI-FINALS OVER THE LAST 15 YEARS

1821 How many All-Ireland semi-finals in a row did Kilkenny reach between 1997 and 2006?

1822 Who scored Waterford's only goal in the 2006 semi-final against Cork?

1823 How many All-Ireland semi-finals did Clare reach between 1995 and 2006 (not including the 1998 replay and second replay)?

1824 Name the Cork midfielder who scored six points in the 2004 semi-final against Wexford.

1825 Who scored Galway's two goals in the 2001 semi-final win over Kilkenny?

1826 Who did Offaly beat in the 1994 semi-final?

1827 Name the Offaly midfielder who scored 0-7 in the 2000 semi-final against Cork.

1828 What year did Down last contest an All-Ireland semi-final?

1829 Who did Galway beat in the 1993 semi-final?

1830 What year did two Munster teams first contest an All-Ireland semi-final against each other?

ANSWERS PAGE 221

1831 Prior to 2007, when was the last time a semi-final ended in a draw and who were the participants?

1832 Prior to 2007, when was the last time a semi-final failed to produce a goal and who were the participants?

1833 What year did Antrim last contest a semi-final?

1834 How many All-Ireland semi-finals did Cork contest between 1999 and 2006 inclusive?

1835 Who scored Kilkenny's only goal in the 2002 semi-final against Tipperary?

1836 Mattie Murphy managed Galway (senior) to how many All-Ireland semi-finals in the last 15 years?

1837 Who was the Tipperary manager for the 2003 semi-final against Kilkenny?

1838 Name the Waterford player who scored 0-13 in the 2004 semi-final against Kilkenny.

1839 Who scored Kilkenny's only goal in the 1998 semi-final against Waterford?

1840 Who was the Galway goalkeeper in the 1996 semi-final against Wexford?

ANSWERS PAGE 221

GENERAL KNOWLEDGE

1841 How many Connacht football finals did Sligo contest between 2002 and 2007 (inclusive)?

1842 Who managed the Carlow footballers in the 2007 championship?

1843 Name the former goalkeeper who won seven All-Ireland Poc Fada competitions in a row between 1984 and 1990.

1844 How many Leinster football semi-finals did Wexford contest between 2004 and 2007 (inclusive)?

1845 What year was the International Rules (Compromise) Series first played between Ireland and Australia?

1846 Who managed the International Rules Team to success in 2004?

1847 Mark McCrory, who played midfield on the St Gall's team that contested the 2006 All-Ireland club final, played inter-county football with which two counties?

1848 Who managed the International Rules Team to success in 2001?

1849 The great Kerry team of 1975-86 played in 11 All-Ireland semi-finals. How many did they win?

1850 Who were the two Mayo players selected on the GAA's Football Team of the Millennium?

ANSWERS PAGE 221

1851 The scoreline was 4-15 to 4-10 in an All-Ireland football semi-final in the last 30 years. Name the teams and the year.

1852 Who managed the International Rules Team to success in 1999?

1853 How many games did Meath play in the 1991 Leinster championship?

1854 Name the Antrim footballer who was named 'Player of the Tournament' in the 2007 Sigerson Cup Weekend.

1855 Who managed the International Rules Team to success in 1986?

1856 Name the hurling club in Mayo that won 22 county titles in a 24-year period between 1978 and 2001.

1857 Who are the only club in the country to win 13 county football titles in a row?

1858 Name the hurling club in Donegal that won 15 county titles in a row between 1991 and 2005.

1859 Name the Wicklow hurler who won All-Ireland Poc Fada titles in 1997 and 2000.

1860 Who were Dublin's three goalscorers in the classic 1977 All-Ireland semi-final against Kerry?

LEADING 20 GOALSCORERS IN SENIOR HURLING CHAMPIONSHIPS FROM 1930 TO 2006

1861 Name the legendary Wexford player who scored 60 goals in 36 championship matches.

1862 Name the Wexford player who scored 40 goals in a period ranging from the late 1960s to the mid 1980s.

1863 Name the Cork corner-forward from the three-in-a-row All-Ireland winning team of the 1970s who hit 38 goals.

1864 Name the legendary Kilkenny player who made the GAA's Team of the Millennium who hit 36 goals in 50 championship matches.

1865 Name the Kilkenny hurler from the last 20 years to hit 34 goals.

1866 Name the legendary Cork hurler from the GAA's Team of the Millennium who hit 33 goals.

1867 Paddy McMahon hit 31 championship goals in 31 games but which county did he play for?

1868 Paddy Lawlor scored 30 championship goals in 24 games but which county did he play for?

1869 Name the legendary Limerick hurler who scored 29 goals in 42 games.

1870 Name the former Cork All-Ireland winning captain who hit 28 goals.

1871 Name the Limerick hurler who played in the 1973, 1974 and 1980 All-Ireland finals who hit 27 goals in 39 games.

1872 Name the Offaly hurler who hit 25 goals in just 24 championship matches.

1873 Name the former Cork dual player All-Ireland medal winner who finished his career in 1986 and who hit 24 goals in 40 games.

1874 Tim Flood is the 12th leading goalscorer between 1930 and 2006 but how many All-Irelands did he win with Wexford?

1875 Ted O'Sullivan has the best goal average of all time with 22 goals in just 12 games but for which county did he play?

1876 Pat Delaney from Kilkenny hit 22 goals but how many All-Ireland senior titles did he win?

1877 Name the former Kilkenny All-Ireland winning captain from the last 15 years who hit 21 goals in 31 games.

1878 Who is the only hurler still playing who is in the top 20 goalscorers between 1930 and 2006?

1879 Name the former Cork forward who was still playing up to 15 years ago who hit 21 goals in 40 games.

1880 Name the Tipperary player who was still playing up until just over a decade ago who hit 20 goals in 35 championship games.

ANSWERS PAGE 221

CLASSIC FOOTBALL AND HURLING MATCHES OVER THE LAST 15 YEARS

1881 Who scored the winning point for Mayo in the 2006 All-Ireland football semi-final against Dublin?

1882 How many goals were scored in the 2007 Waterford-Cork Munster hurling semi-final?

1883 Who scored Armagh's goal against Tyrone from an acute angle in the classic 2005 All-Ireland semi-final?

1884 Who managed Offaly in the 1996 Leinster hurling final?

1885 Who did Kildare defeat in a classic qualifier game in Newbridge in 2001?

1886 The scoreline was 2-16 to 2-5 but which provincial hurling final over the last 15 years is still regarded as one of the greatest games of all time?

1887 Who scored Armagh's last point in the 2002 All-Ireland football final?

1888 How many goals were scored in the epic Galway-Kilkenny 2005 All-Ireland semi-final?

1889 Who was the Derry coach who gave an impassioned speech at half-time to the players in the 1993 All-Ireland semi-final against Dublin?

1890 Which two teams played out a classic All-Ireland hurling semi-final in 1999 on a scoreline of 0-19 to 0-16?

ANSWERS PAGE 222

1891 Name the Cork player who scored a classy soccer-type solo goal in the opening minutes of the 2001 Munster final between Cork and Kerry.

1892 Who scored Clare's winning point in the 1997 All-Ireland hurling final against Tipperary?

1893 Name the Armagh substitute who scored the critical second goal for Armagh in the 2002 replayed Ulster quarter-final againt Tyrone?

1894 Who was the Galway goalkeeper in the 1999 drawn All-Ireland hurling quarter-final against Clare?

1895 Who scored Derry's goal in the 1993 All-Ireland final against Cork?

1896 Who were Cork's two goalscorers in the epic drawn All-Ireland hurling semi-final between Cork and Wexford in 2003?

1897 When Galway played Mayo in the 1997 Connacht championship, who was the Galway manager who played that day?

1898 Who got Kilkenny's equalising point after the ball was worked up the field from the full-back line in the 1993 drawn Leinster hurling final against Wexford?

1899 Who scored the winning goal for Down in their classic Ulster football clash against Derry in 1994?

1900 Who was the Cork goalscorer in the 2004 Munster hurling final between Cork and Waterford?

ANSWERS PAGE 222

GENERAL KNOWLEDGE

1901 The old Liam MacCarthy Cup was replaced by a new trophy, also the Liam MacCarthy Cup, in which year?

1902 Name the only hurler in history to win nine Senior inter-county All-Ireland medals.

1903 Name the only two hurlers in history to win eight All-Ireland medals on the field of play.

1904 Before Liam Mulvihill took over as GAA Ard Stiurthoir in 1979, who was his immediate predecessor?

1905 Who were the two Roscommon GAA Presidents?

1906 Name the five Kerry players from the great team of 1975-86 that won eight All-Ireland medals and who hold the record for the most All-Ireland medals won.

1907 Only two Kerry players who won eight All-Irelands started and finished every one of those eight final successes. Name them.

1908 Name the only player in history to win All-Ireland minor, U-21 and senior medals in football and hurling.

1909 Name the only player to have won 11 consecutive Munster senior titles (hurling and football).

1910 Which college did Clare's Frank Lohan captain to Fitzgibbon Cup success in 1996?

1911 Mick Malone is the only player to win four All-Ireland U-21 medals but which county did he win them with?

1912 Who was the first Antrim hurler to be selected as an All-Star?

1913 Which family hold the record number of All-Ireland medals won in either hurling or football with 19?

1914 Name the only Kerry hurler to win a Railway Cup medal on the field of play (he won it in the last 15 years).

1915 Who did Muhammad Ali (Cassius Clay) fight in Croke Park in July 1973?

1916 What year was the new Sam Maguire Cup presented to the winners of the All-Ireland senior title?

1917 The first Munster championship football game televised live in 1993 featured a game between which two teams?

1918 Name the two Cork players who played in four Munster senior finals on successive Sundays in 1987.

1919 Name the two brothers who played on opposing teams in the 1981 Munster hurling semi-final between Limerick and Tipperary.

1920 Between 1997 and 2007, Clare played Cork seven times in the hurling championship but Clare scored only two goals in those seven games. Name the two goalscorers.

ANSWERS PAGE 222

LEGENDARY SCORING FEATS AND SCORERS IN HURLING AND FOOTBALL

1921 Who is the highest championship scorer in hurling history?

1922 The second highest championship scorer in hurling history is still playing the game. Name him.

1923 Name the Offaly footballer who scored 2-9 (2-3 from play) in the 1980 All-Ireland semi-final against Kerry.

1924 Who holds the record for the highest score in an All-Ireland hurling final?

1925 Name the Dublin player who holds the joint record for the highest score in an All-Ireland football final.

1926 Name the Kerry player who holds the joint record for the highest score in an All-Ireland football final.

1927 Name the Wexford hurler who scored a record total of 7-7 against Antrim in the 1954 All-Ireland semi-final.

1928 Name the Galway hurler who scored 2-10 in the replayed 1999 All-Ireland quarter-final.

1929 Name the hurler who hit 7-74 in ten All-Ireland final appearances.

1930 Name Offaly's highest championship scorer in their hurling history.

1931 What score did Mattie Forde hit for Wexford in the 2004 All-Ireland football qualifiers against Offaly?

1932 Name the Cork hurler (apart from Christy Ring) who is the sixth highest championship scorer in history with 28-153.

1933 Which player holds the highest individual score in the Ulster football championship with 3-9 in a game against Monaghan in 2002?

1934 Name the Kerry player from the 1970s and 1980s who hit nine goals in All-Ireland football semi-finals.

1935 Tom Carew hit 0-16 for his county in a 2001 hurling championship game (including extra-time) but which county did he play for?

1936 Name the Offaly player who hit 3-8 against Kilkenny in the 1989 Leinster hurling final.

1937 Name the Limerick hurler who hit 5-3 against Tipperary in the 1936 Munster final.

1938 Name the Leitrim player who hit 2-13 against London in the 1997 Connacht championship.

1939 Name the Clare player who scored 6-4 against Limerick in the 1953 Munster championship.

1940 Name the Galway footballer who hit a record (in an All-Ireland final) 2-5 from play in the 1956 All-Ireland final against Cork.

GENERAL KNOWLEDGE

1941 Who are the only father and son to win hurling All-Star awards?

1942 Who scored the winning point for Clare deep in stoppage time of their 2002 All-Ireland hurling quarter-final win against Galway?

1943 Prior to 2007, name the only player in history to win All-Star hurling awards in four different lines of the pitch (full-back line, half-back line, midfield and half-forward line).

1944 Only two hurlers have won five All-Stars before they were 24. Name them.

1945 Name the two sets of cousins (on opposite sides) who played in the 2001 Munster hurling final.

1946 Name the last Ulster hurler to win an All-Star award.

1947 Name the only footballer to win four Texaco awards for Footballer of the Year.

1948 Name the former GAA President who refereed All-Ireland hurling and football finals in 1960.

1949 Name the only player to captain All-Ireland minor and senior winning football teams.

1950 Only three players in history have captained All-Ireland U-21 and All-Ireland senior winning teams. Denis 'Ogie' Moran was the first but can you name the other two?

ANSWERS PAGE 223

1951 Name the Thurles Sarsfields and former Tipperary player who was top scorer in three Fitzgibbon Cup finals between 1996 and 1999.

1952 Joe Cassells captained Meath to the All-Ireland title after the 1988 final replay. Who captained them in the drawn game?

1953 When was an All-Ireland hurling semi-final last played outside of Croke Park and where was the venue?

1954 Name the Offaly player who hit 1-17 in four All-Ireland hurling finals between 1994 and 2000.

1955 How many All-Ireland hurling finals did Kilkenny contest in the 1970s?

1956 Prior to 2007, name the only footballer to win Provincial Senior medals and a Tommy Murphy Cup medal.

1957 In the last 20 years, who is the only man to captain an All-Ireland winning team and manage a county to an All-Ireland final?

1958 Who was the last player to play in All-Ireland senior hurling and football finals in the same year?

1959 The last hurler to win three All-Ireland minor medals achieved his feat in the last 25 years. Name him.

1960 Only four hurlers captained their county to All-Ireland minor and All-Ireland senior titles. Name three of them.

ANSWERS PAGE 223

PROVINCIAL AND ALL-IRELAND CLUB HURLING

1961 What year did Birr win their first All-Ireland club title?

1962 Who are the only Ulster club to win the All-Ireland club title?

1963 Which team has lost three Leinster club finals this decade?

1964 How many Munster club finals did Mount Sion and Ballygunner (combined) contest between 1999 and 2005 (inclusive)?

1965 Who were the first Galway club to win an All-Ireland title?

1966 Which club has lost five All-Ireland club finals?

1967 Which Antrim club were Ulster club champions in 2004?

1968 Who did Newtownshandrum defeat in the 2004 All-Ireland semi-final after a replay?

1969 Name the inter-county manager who managed Clarinbridge to the 2002 All-Ireland final.

1970 Who are the only Wexford club to have won an All-Ireland title?

1971 Which two teams fought out a mammoth battle in the 1992 All-Ireland semi-final that went to three games?

ANSWERS PAGE 223

1972 Which Limerick club did Sarsfields defeat in the 1993 All-Ireland final?

1973 Which Clare club contested five Munster club finals between 1992 and 2002?

1974 What year did Simon Whelehan captain Birr to an All-Ireland title?

1975 Who were the last Dublin club to reach a Leinster club final in 1996?

1976 Which Clare club did Birr defeat after extra-time in a replay of the 1998 All-Ireland semi-final?

1977 Name the two Roscommon clubs to have won Connacht club hurling titles.

1978 In the 1993 Munster club final between Sixmilebridge and Toomevara, the Toomevara coach had to step down before that final because he was playing for Sixmilebridge. Name him.

1979 In the last 20 years, two clubs that won All-Ireland club titles were relegated to Intermediate grade within five years. Name the two clubs.

1980 Who is the only player in history to captain three All-Ireland winning club teams?

GENERAL KNOWLEDGE

1981 Name the Limerick hurler who coached University of Limerick to the 2002 Fitzgibbon Cup title but who won a Fitzgibbon Cup medal with Waterford Institute of Technology a year later.

1982 Paddy Ruschitzko captained which county to their last provincial hurling success?

1983 Peter Canavan scored 11 points out of Tyrone's total of 0-12 in the 1995 All-Ireland final. Who scored their other point?

1984 Who are the only brothers to win All-Stars in hurling and football?

1985 Who was the last captain to receive a trophy in the old Hogan Stand before it was demolished in 1999?

1986 What year was the first Hurling-Shinty international staged between Ireland and Scotland after the Camanachd association re-established links with the GAA?

1987 In the 1994 All-Ireland minor final against Cork, the Galway goalkeeper had the unique distinction of having never touched the ball once during the entire game (including puckouts). Name him.

1988 What year was the All-Ireland club hurling semi-finals and final staged over a weekend?

1989 Ronan McGarrity played in three All-Ireland Senior football finals over the last 15 years. Name those three years.

1990 Name the Galway player who scored 1-10 in the 2003 All-Ireland minor hurling final against Kilkenny and still ended up on the losing side.

1991 Name the current inter-county hurler who is the only player over the last 27 years to win Fitzgibbon and Sigerson Cup medals.

1992 Who were the last county to achieve a hurling treble by winning All-Ireland senior, U-21 and minor titles in the same season? Name the year also.

1993 What player held the top scorer record in Ulster Senior football from 1971 until it was finally beaten in 2005?

1994 Which player beat that above record in 2005?

1995 Name the Wexford player who scored the equalising goal with the last puck of the game in the drawn 2003 All-Ireland semi-final against Cork.

1996 Which player won a Dublin county football medal with UCD in 2006 but subsequently played against them four weeks later in a Leinster club semi-final?

1997 Name the only two hurlers to win ten Munster senior medals each?

1998 Who was the first player to receive a yellow card when the GAA introduced the practise for the first time during the 1998-99 National Football League?

ANSWERS PAGE 223

1999 True or false. Tipperary v Limerick in the 2007 Munster hurling championship was the only time in hurling championship history that two teams finished level after extra-time in a replay and the second replay also required extra-time.

2000 Since the millennium, name the player who scored a goal in the All-Ireland senior hurling final but who had yet to play senior championship hurling with his own club.

ANSWERS

GENERAL KNOWLEDGE – page 8

1 Nemo Rangers (seven titles). **2** The Bomber. **3** Young Irelands, Gowran.
4 Armagh. **5** Rule 42. **6** Mickey Harte. **7** Seamus Darby. **8** Five. **9** John
Fenton. **10** Thurles. **11** Sean Og O hAilpin. **12** Teddy McCarthy (Cork).
13 Queen's University Belfast. **14** Limerick IT. **15** Dessie Farrell. **16** Paraic
Duffy. **17** Kieran McGeeney. **18** Nickey Brennan. **19** Ambrose O'Donovan.
20 Conor Hayes (Galway), Anthony Daly (Clare) and Liam Fennelly
(Kilkenny).

FOOTBALL GENERAL KNOWLEDGE – page 10

21 1947. **22** Maurice Fitzgerald. **23** Dermot Earley. **24** Philip Clifford.
25 1994. **26** Four. **27** John Maughan. **28** Four. **29** 2001. **30** 2004. **31** Cork.
32 Kevin O'Brien (1990). **33** Martin O'Connell (Meath). **34** Kildare.
35 John O'Leary. **36** 2001. **37** Frank McGuigan. **38** John Rafferty.
39 Kieran Donaghy. **40** Keith Higgins.

MANAGERIAL ROLL CALL 1 – page 12

41 Four (Kerry, Kildare, Laois, Wicklow). **42** Three. **43** Three. **44** Diarmuid
Healy. **45** Eamonn Coleman. **46** Three. **47** Four. **48** Four. **49** Pat
Henderson. **50** Four. **51** Brian McEniff. **52** Eugene McGee. **53** Laois.
54 Pete McGrath. **55** Ollie Walsh. **56** Three (Kerry, Westmeath, Clare).
57 Canon Bertie Troy. **58** Father Tom Gilhooly. **59** Seven. **60** Tony
Hanahoe (Dublin – 1977).

HURLING GENERAL KNOWLEDGE – page 14

61 Mark O'Leary. **62** Sarsfields (Galway). **63** Liam Donoghue. **64** 1998.
65 1973. **66** Sean Delargy. **67** Pat Fleury. **68** Brian Whelehan. **69** 1998.
70 2003. **71** Offaly. **72** Jim Nelson. **73** John Allen. **74** Bobby Ryan.
75 Seven. **76** 3-3. **77** Fergal Ryan. **78** 2000. **79** Three. **80** Two (1999 and
2004).

DUAL PLAYERS – page 16

81 Sean Og O hAilpin. **82** Darren Rooney. **83** Six (five hurling and one football). **84** Liam Currams. **85** 1993. **86** Kildare. **87** Greg Blaney. **88** David Tierney. **89** 1972. **90** Kieran McKeever. **91** Jack Lynch (Cork). **92** Keith Higgins. **93** Brendan Cummins. **94** Stephen Lucey. **95** Denis Walsh. **96** Denis Coughlan. **97** Leonard McGrath (hurling in 1923 and football in 1925). **98** Paddy Mackey. **99** 1975. **100** Ray Cummins (Cork – 1971).

ALL-IRELAND SENIOR HURLING FINALS – page 18

101 Willie O'Connor. **102** Six. **103** Joe Errity and Brian Whelehan. **104** Eugene Cloonan and Fergal Healy. **105** 1990 (Cork). **106** Six. **107** Tom Cashman. **108** Tom Dempsey (1-3). **109** Eamonn Taaffe. **110** 1938. **111** 1972. **112** Birr. **113** 1931. **114** Killarney in 1937. **115** Conor Gleeson. **116** True. **117** Andy and Martin Comerford (Kilkenny). **118** It was the first time a goal wasn't scored in an All-Ireland senior final. **119** Art Foley. **120** Tyler Mackey (1910) and Mick Mackey (1936 and 1940).

FOOTBALL GENERAL KNOWLEDGE – page 20

121 Jody Devine. **122** Declan Browne. **123** Tommy Murphy. **124** Peter Canavan. **125** Ten. **126** Brian Dooher. **127** Benny Tierney. **128** Gary Fahey. **129** Alan Brogan. **130** Ray Silke. **131** Tommy Dowd. **132** Roscommon. **133** 1-15 to 0-17. **134** Padraig Joyce and Paul Clancy. **135** 1957. **136** Three. **137** Brian McIver. **138** Cormac Bane. **139** Tyrone and Roscommon. **140** Tipperary v Louth in 2001 (the game started earlier than the rest of the games that evening).

FAMINE ENDINGS – page 22

141 1981. **142** 32. **143** Antrim. **144** Galway hurlers. **145** 1914. **146** Laois. **147** Westmeath. **148** 65. **149** 28. **150** 1981. **151** Fermanagh. **152** Derry hurlers. **153** 1982. **154** 1956. **155** Cavan. **156** Down. **157** 39. **158** Offaly. **159** 19. **160** Richard Stakelum.

ALL-IRELAND FINAL BAND OF BROTHERS – page 24

161 Declan Carr (Tipperary – 1991), Tommy Carr (Dublin – 1992). **162** Two. **163** Eddie and Willie O'Connor (1993 and 2000). **164** Two. **165** Tommy and Padraig Joyce, Gary and Richie Fahey. **166** Brian and Frank Lohan, Colm and Conal Bonnar. **167** Ben and Jerry O'Connor (Cork), John and

Tony McEntee (Armagh), Dave and Rod Guiney (Wexford). **168** Joe, Johnny and Billy Dooley, Brian and Simon Whelehan, Gary and Darren Hannify. **169** John and Tony McEntee, Justin and Enda McNulty. **170** James and Martin McHugh. **171** Pascal and Peter Canavan, Chris and Stephen Lawn. **172** Padraig and Tommy Joyce, Michael and John Donnellan, Declan and Tomas Meehan, Gary and Richie Fahey. **173** Mick, Tom and Pat Spillane, Darragh, Tomas and Marc O Se (All Kerry). **174** Sean and Owen O'Neill, Mike and Declan Nash. **175** Finbarr and Pascal McConnell (Tyrone). **176** Paul and Eoin Kelly, Alan and Mark Kerins. **177** Brian, Barry and Simon Whelehan (2000). **178** Ben and Jerry O'Connor, Donal Og and Conor Cusack. **179** Henry and Seamus Downey, Damien and Fergal McCusker, Tony and Don Davis. **180** Five (Mick and Pat Fitzgerald, Seamus and Stephen Darby, Matt and Richie Connor, Liam and Tomas O'Connor, Sean and Brendan Lowry).

GENERAL KNOWLEDGE – page 26
181 St Kieran's. **182** Limerick. **183** Cormac McAnallen. **184** Thurles Sarsfields. **185** Maurice Davin. **186** Michael 'Babs' Keating. **187** 18. **188** Graham Geraghty. **189** 1992. **190** 1989. **191** His brother Mike. **192** Dara O Cinneide. **193** Pat Roe. **194** Sligo Rovers' FAI Cup final success. **195** Connacht. **196** Clare. **197** Westmeath. **198** London. **199** Tipperary. **200** Tony Wall.

TRUE OR FALSE – page 28
201 False. **202** True. **203** True. **204** True. **205** False (he plays with Na Piarsaigh). **206** False (they lost all 11 finals). **207** True. **208** False (they won eight in a row). **209** True (Ballyhale Shamrocks v Toomevara in 2007). **210** False. **211** False (they were beaten in the final by Limerick). **212** True. **213** True (1957). **214** False (they didn't win any). **215** True. **216** False (he captained them to the 1982 title). **217** False (they have won one). **218** False. **219** True. **220** False.

NAME THE YEAR 1 – page 30
221 1980. **222** 2003. **223** 2002. **224** 2002. **225** 1998. **226** 1995. **227** 1997. **228** 2001. **229** 2001. **230** 2002. **231** 2006. **232** 2003. **233** 2005. **234** 2000. **235** 1995. **236** 2000. **237** 2003. **238** 2006. **239** 1993. **240** 1989.

GENERAL KNOWLEDGE – page 32
241 1992. **242** UCD. **243** Rower Inistioge. **244** The Cooley Mountains.
245 Eamonn Cregan. **246** Colm Cooper. **247** Michael Bond. **248** Damien
Fox. **249** 1995. **250** Cork. **251** Pat Holmes. **252** Stephen O'Neill (Tyrone).
253 Ten. **254** Ger Farragher (Galway). **255** Padraig Nolan. **256** Declan
Darcy. **257** 1998. **258** Fermanagh and Wicklow. **259** Peter Canavan.
260 23.

REFEREES – page 34
261 Wexford. **262** Cavan. **263** Tipperary. **264** Longford. **265** Tipperary
(formerly of Wexford). **266** Cork. **267** Cork. **268** Dublin. **269** Westmeath.
270 Monaghan. **271** Kerry. **272** Waterford. **273** Clare. **274** Sligo.
275 Limerick. **276** Cork. **277** Tipperary. **278** Galway. **279** Mayo.
280 Offaly.

**TEXACO HURLER AND FOOTBALLER OF THE YEAR OVER THE LAST
15 YEARS**
HURLING – page 35
281 1996. **282** Jamesie O'Connor. **283** 1992 and 1999. **284** Sean
McMahon. **285** 2002. **286** 1994 and 1998. **287** JJ Delaney. **288** Sean Og
O hAilpin. **289** Jerry O'Connor. **290** Tommy Dunne.
FOOTBALL – page 36
291 1994. **292** Paul Curran. **293** Peter Canavan. **294** Martin McHugh.
295 Maurice Fitzgerald. **296** 1999. **297** Colm Cooper. **298** Michael
Donnellan. **299** Padraig Joyce. **300** Seamus Moynihan.

CLUB HURLERS – page 37
301 JK Brackens. **302** Ballyhale Shamrocks. **303** Grenagh. **304** Ardmore.
305 Rapparees. **306** Ballyskenagh. **307** Corofin. **308** Liam Mellowes.
309 Lismore. **310** O'Toole's. **311** Carrickshock. **312** Ahane. **313** Tinnahinch.
314 Castlelyons. **315** Loughgiel Shamrocks. **316** Wolfe Tones.
317 Emeralds. **318** Passage. **319** St Martin's. **320** Tynagh-Abbey-Duniry.

GENERAL KNOWLEDGE – page 38
321 David Heaney. **322** Pat Mulcahy. **323** Stephen O'Neill. **324** Michael
Haverty. **325** Limerick Institute of Technology (LIT). **326** Brian Whelehan.
327 Paul Flynn. **328** Paddy O'Rourke. **329** Willie O'Dwyer. **330** Terence

and Shane McNaughton (Antrim). **331** Graigue/Ballycallan. **332** Ardboe.
333 Hayes' Hotel. **334** Weeshie Fogarty. **335** Jimmy Doyle. **336** Eugene
McEntee. **337** 1948. **338** Kevin Heffernan. **339** Three. **340** Denis Byrne.

GENERAL KNOWLEDGE – page 40
341 Thurles. **342** Lory Meagher. **343** 2.5 metres. **344** Five (Connacht,
Leinster, Munster, Ulster, Britain). **345** April. **346** Powerscreen.
347 Sixteen. **348** Gael Linn. **349** Dublin. **350** Three. **351** Christy Ring
Trophy. **352** Archbishop of Cashel, Dermot Clifford. **353** Boston.
354 Castleblayney Faughs. **355** Charlie Redmond. **356** Offaly.
357 Belfast. **358** London. **359** John O Leary and Graham Geraghty.
360 Three (Nemo, Laune and Crossmaglen).

ALL-IRELAND FOOTBALL SEMI-FINALS – page 42
361 Kerry. **362** Ray Cosgrove. **363** Seven. **364** Offaly. **365** Five. **366** Steven
McDonnell and Oisin McConville. **367** Kildare. **368** Five. **369** Mayo.
370 Cork. **371** 1983 (Cork v Dublin replay). **372** Mickey Moran. **373**
Johnny McGurk. **374** Larry Tompkins. **375** Dara O Cinneide. **376** 2002,
Kerry v Cork. **377** 2003, Armagh v Donegal. **378** 2001, Galway v Derry.
379 Cork (1993). **380** Dublin (1974-79).

PAST COUNTY HURLERS – page 44
381 Midleton. **382** Ballygunner. **383** Bennettsbridge. **384** Lattin-Cullen.
385 Kiltormer. **386** Oulart-the-Ballagh. **387** St Finbarr's. **388** Clarecastle.
389 Bruree. **390** James Stephens. **391** Seir Kieran. **392** Kinvara.
393 Cushendall. **394** Mullinahone. **395** Patrickswell. **396** Fenians,
Johnstown. **397** Portlaoise. **398** St Martins and O'Tooles. **399** Portaferry.
400 Bodyke.

ALL-IRELAND MINOR HURLING AND FOOTBALL CAPTAINS OVER THE LAST 15 YEARS – page 45
401 Galway hurlers. **402** Roscommon footballers. **403** 1994. **404** Down.
405 Galway. **406** 1992. **407** 1995. **408** 2004. **409** 2000. **410** 2002.
411 Richie Power. **412** 2000. **413** 2001. **414** Derry. **415** Laois footballers.
416 Laois footballers in 1997. **417** Damien Gavin. **418** Tipperary (1996).
419 John Reddan. **420** Dan O'Neill.

GENERAL KNOWLEDGE – page 47

421 Ahane. **422** Two. **423** The Artane Boys' Band. **424** Kenneth Burke. **425** 1993 and 2000. **426** Keith Higgins. **427** Glenmore. **428** Castletown. **429** 1993. **430** Mark Vaughan. **431** Anthony Nash. **432** Brian Mullins. **433** Na Fianna. **434** Two. **435** 1915. **436** Ger Loughnane. **437** Eoin, Patrick and TJ Reid (Ballyhale Shamrocks). **438** Michael Meehan and Sean Armstrong. **439** Des Foley. **440** Pat Dunny.

FIRSTS – page 49

441 2007. **442** 1992. **443** Down. **444** Sarsfields. **445** 1986. **446** UCD. **447** 1973. **448** 1973. **449** 1980. **450** 1992. **451** 2002. **452** 1991 (The year he began his presidency). **453** Jim Wall (1972). **454** Limerick. **455** Paddy O'Rourke. **456** Dublin and Tyrone in 2007 National League. **457** 2000. **458** 1981. **459** Kevin Mussen (Down). **460** WJ Spain (a native of Tipperary, he won football in 1887 with Limerick and hurling in 1889 with Dublin).

MUNSTER SENIOR HURLING FINALS – page 51

461 Ken McGrath. **462** Six. **463** Three. **464** Five. **465** Five. **466** 1996. **467** Sean O'Connor. **468** Pa O'Neill. **469** 1938. **470** 1970. **471** John Mullane. **472** 1996. **473** Gary Kirby. **474** Ger 'Redser' O'Grady. **475** 1987, '88 and '89. **476** Kieran McGuckian. **477** Joe McKenna. **478** Seanie O'Leary. **479** Tony O'Sullivan. **480** Eoin O'Neill.

CLUBCALL 1 – page 53

481 Donegal. **482** Clare. **483** Antrim. **484** Louth. **485** Wexford. **486** Louth. **487** Armagh. **488** Waterford. **489** Carlow. **490** Kilkenny. **491** Sligo. **492** Dublin. **493** Laois. **494** Longford. **495** Offaly. **496** Westmeath. **497** Tipperary. **498** Cavan. **499** Limerick. **500** Kerry.

GAA PLAYERS WHO PLAYED OTHER CODES – page 54

501 Kevin Moran. **502** Dave Barry. **503** 1983. **504** Tipperary. **505** Kerry. **506** Wimbledon. **507** Armagh. **508** Nottingham Forest. **509** Anthony Tohill. **510** Graham Geraghty. **511** Salthill/Knocknacarra. **512** Liam McHale. **513** Galway. **514** Clare. **515** Hockey. **516** Michael Donnellan. **517** Kevin Walsh. **518** Brendan Devenney. **519** UCC. **520** Offaly.

FOOTBALL GENERAL KNOWLEDGE – page 56

521 Mickey Quinn. **522** Mick Brewster. **523** Enda Colleran and Sean Purcell. **524** Paul Brady. He and Michael Finnegan retained the All-Ireland 40x20 senior doubles handball title and later lined out with Cavan in a League Division 2 semi-final with Cavan. **525** Shane O'Rourke (son of Colm). **526** 1961 All-Ireland football final between Down and Offaly. **527** True. **528** Tyrone. **529** Paidi O Se. **530** Three. **531** Rory O'Connell. **532** Na Fianna. **533** Paddy Cullen. **534** Tourlestrane. **535** St Jarlath's Tuam. **536** Five. **537** Brian McEniff. **538** Martin Daly. **539** Mickey Ned O'Sullivan (Pat Spillane received the trophy because O'Sullivan was carried off injured). **540** Preston North End.

CAPTAINS' PARADE – page 58

541 Anthony Molloy. **542** Gerald McCarthy (Cork) in 1966. **543** Fergal Hartley. **544** Padraig Horan. **545** Packie Cooney (Sarsfields) and Joe Rabbitte (Athenry). **546** Lorcan Hassett. **547** Ian Fitzgerald. **548** Donal O'Grady. **549** Maurice Sheridan. **550** Peter Canavan and Cormac McAnallen (both Tyrone – Canavan in 1991 and 1992 and McAnallen in 2000 and 2001). **551** Andy Maloney (Tipperary/Waterford and Waterford IT – 1999 and 2000). **552** Leonard Enright (Limerick). **553** Ciaran Barr. **554** Ciaran Corr. **555** 1990. **556** Dan Murphy (Cork – 1997 and 1998). **557** Ger and Kevin Fennelly. **558** Jim and Oisin McConville (Crossmaglen Rangers – 1997 and 2007). **559** John Kennedy (Dublin – 1891, 1892, 1894). **560** John Joe Sheehy (1926 and 1930) and Sean Og Sheehy (1962) – both Kerry.

TROPHY PARADE – page 60

561 Leinster senior hurling championship. **562** Irish Press Cup. **563** All-Ireland colleges. **564** Tom Markham Cup. **565** All-Ireland club. **566** Anglo Celt. **567** Andy Merrigan Cup. **568** All-Ireland senior camogie. **569** U-21 hurling. **570** The Nestor Cup. **571** National League. **572** Clarke Cup. **573** New Ireland Cup. **574** Munster football. **575** The Cormac McAnallen Trophy. **576** Ulster hurling championship. **577** Ashbourne. **578** Delaney Cup. **579** Connacht minor football champions. **580** It doesn't have a name.

GAA GROUNDS – page 62
581 Casement Park. **582** Castlebar. **583** Kingspan Breffni Park. **584** St Tiernach's Park. **585** Dungarvan. **586** Newry. **587** Clare and Westmeath. **588** Nenagh. **589** Celtic Park. **590** Omagh. **591** Portlaoise. **592** O'Connor Park. **593** Ballybofey. **594** The Athletic Grounds. **595** Pairc Sheáin MacDiarmada. **596** Carlow. **597** Nowlan Park. **598** Longford. **599** Galway. **600** Ballycran (Down).

NATIONAL HURLING LEAGUE – page 64
601 44. **602** Michael Walsh. **603** Clare. **604** Four. **605** 1978. **606** 1991. **607** Tommy Dunne (Tipperary). **608** Three. **609** Ollie Canning. **610** 1998. **611** None. **612** Tipperary (18 titles). **613** Limerick (five titles in a row between 1934 and 1938). **614** 1992. **615** 1997. **616** They were all out of a managers job the following year. **617** 1973. **618** Christy Ring. **619** Joe Cooney. **620** Henry Shefflin (2-6 in 2006 and 0-12 in 2007).

NICKNAMES – page 66
621 'Cha'. **622** 'Star'. **623** 'Brick'. **624** 'Gizzy'. **625** 'Gooch'. **626** 'Magic'. **627** 'Jayo'. **628** 'Doc'. **629** 'Red'. **630** 'Goggles'. **631** 'Hopper'. **632** 'Sambo'. **633** 'Fan'. **634** 'Boy wonder'. **635** 'Jobber'. **636** 'Tyler'. **637** 'Snitchie'. **638** 'The Gunner'. **639** 'The Bawn'. **640** 'Drug'.

CONNACHT FOOTBALL – page 67
641 Conor Mortimer. **642** 1975. **643** Gerry Lohan. **644** 2000. **645** Four. **646** Galway. **647** Fergal O'Donnell. **648** Matthew Clancy. **649** David Nestor. **650** James Horan. **651** Roscommon (1977-80). **652** Galway. **653** Six. **654** Mayo. **655** Joe Bergin. **656** Michael Donnellan. **657** Derek Duggan. **658** Ja Fallon. **659** Jack O'Shea. **660** Seven.

GENERAL KNOWLEDGE – page 69
661 Cavan. **662** Tommy Sugrue. **663** 1970. **664** 1975. **665** Sarsfields (Galway), Dunloy (Antrim), St Joseph's Doora-Barefield (Clare), Athenry (Galway), Birr (Offaly). **666** UCC and Tralee IT. **667** Good Counsel, New Ross. **668** Jimmy Barry Murphy. **669** Carlow. **670** Five. **671** 1991. **672** Clare. **673** Meath. **674** Portlaoise (football, 1983). **675** Wexford. **676** Pat Nally. **677** Monaleen. **678** John Owens (Tipperary). **679** 'Tough'. **680** Kilkenny.

HURLERS IN ALL-IRELAND FINALS IN THE LAST 15 YEARS – page 71
681 Offaly. **682** Kilkenny. **683** Kilkenny. **684** Clare. **685** Tipperary.
686 Wexford. **687** Cork. **688** Clare. **689** Tipperary. **690** Clare.
691 Galway. **692** Offaly. **693** Wexford. **694** Galway. **695** Kilkenny.
696 Cork. **697** Galway. **698** Cork. **699** Offaly. **700** Galway.

GENERAL KNOWLEDGE – page 72
701 Brian Feeney. **702** Frank and Brian McGuigan. **703** John Meyler.
704 Brian Whelehan. **705** Gary Hanniffy. **706** Down. **707** Mattie Forde.
708 Graigue-Ballycallan. **709** Graham Geraghty. **710** Galway. **711** 1988.
712 Tyrone. **713** Joe Cooney and Pete Finnerty. **714** Derry. **715** Eugene
'Nudie' Hughes. **716** John Kiely. **717** Damien Murray. **718** Dermot Earley
Senior (Roscommon), Dermot Earley Jnr (Kildare). **719** Antrim
Intermediates. **720** Bray Emmet's won the title for Dublin.

**PROVINCIAL AND ALL-IRELAND CLUB FOOTBALL CHAMPIONSHIPS
OVER THE LAST 20 YEARS** – page 74
721 Baltinglass. **722** Dr Crokes. **723** Cathal McGinley. **724** Na Fianna.
725 Colin Corkery. **726** Kilmacud Crokes (1995). **727** Doonbeg.
728 Burren (1986 and 1988). **729** Eire Og, Carlow. **730** Clann na nGael
(Roscommon). **731** Wicklow. **732** Kilmurry-Ibrickane. **733** Knockmore
(Mayo). **734** Stradbally. **735** 2006. **736** St Finbarr's. **737** Brian Ruane.
738 Erins Isle (Dublin). **739** Pat O'Shea (played with Dr Crokes in 1992
and managed Dr Crokes in 2007). John Maughan (played with Castlebar
Mitchel's in 1994 and managed Crossmolina in 2003). Fergal O Se (came
on as a substitute with An Ghaeltacht in 2004 when he was also the
manager). Donal Murtagh (played with Crossmaglen in 1997, 1999 and
2000 and managed the team in 2007). **740** Billy Morgan (Nemo Rangers
and Cork), Tony Hanahoe (St Vincent's and Dublin), Ray Silke (Corofin
and Galway).

ALL-IRELAND FOOTBALL FINALS IN THE LAST 15 YEARS – page 76
741 2000. **742** Pat McEnaney. **743** 2003. **744** Trevor Giles. **745** Ollie
Murphy. **746** DJ Kane. **747** Conor Martin. **748** Three. **749** Owen Mulligan.
750 Noel Connelly. **751** Pat O'Neill. **752** Henry Downey. **753** Pete
McGrath. **754** Brendan Reilly. **755** Joe Kavanagh and John O'Driscoll.
756 Dara O Cinneide. **757** Tommy Howard. **758** Colm Cooper (2004).

759 John O'Leary (Dublin), Noel Connelly (Mayo), Kieran McGeeney (Armagh), Declan O'Sullivan (Kerry). **760** Joe Kavanagh (1993 and 1999), Colm Cooper (2004 and 2006).

CAMOGIE AND LADIES' FOOTBALL FROM THE LAST 15 YEARS
CAMOGIE – page 78
761 Cork. **762** Cork and Tipperary. **763** 1999. **764** 1996. **765** Tipperary (1999-2001). **766** 2004. **767** Dublin. **768** 1994. **769** Kathleen Mills. **770** Deirdre Hughes (Tipperary).
LADIES' FOOTBALL – page 79
771 Cork. **772** Armagh. **773** Waterford. **774** 2004. **775** Four. **776** Monaghan. **777** Dublin. **778** 2005. **779** Diane O'Hora. **780** Mary Kirwan.

ULSTER GENERAL KNOWLEDGE – page 80
781 Bellaghy, Ballinderry, The Loup, Dungiven. **782** 1995. **783** 1993. **784** Jarlath Burns. **785** Five. **786** Ballygalget (2005). **787** Portumna. **788** Sean McCague. **789** IT Sligo. **790** Queen's and Jordanstown. **791** Derry. **792** Brian McAlinden and Brian Canavan. **793** IT Sligo. **794** Cavan. **795** Frank Dawson. **796** Ciaran McKeever. **797** Mount Sion. **798** Jody Gormley. **799** Paul McCormack. **800** 1982.

FORMER COUNTY FOOTBALLERS AND THEIR CLUBS – page 82
801 Mayobridge. **802** O'Donovan Rossa. **803** Austin Stacks. **804** O'Dwyers. **805** An Cheathru Rua. **806** Beale. **807** Summerhill. **808** Ballina Stephenites. **809** Mullaghbawn. **810** Skryne. **811** Swatragh. **812** Rathmore and Clooney-Quin (Clare). **813** Crossmaglen Rangers. **814** Castlehaven. **815** St Mary's, Cahirciveen. **816** Nemo Rangers. **817** An Ghaeltacht. **818** Roscommon Gaels. **819** Killanin. **820** Baltinglass.

INTERPROVINCIAL CHAMPIONSHIPS – PLAYERS INVOLVED OVER THE LAST 15 YEARS – page 83
821 Martin Donnelly. **822** Derry. **823** Enda Murphy. **824** Anthony Daly and Brian Lohan. **825** Conal Keaney. **826** Cork. **827** Christy Byrne. **828** Ollie Moran. **829** Laois. **830** Wexford. **831** Ricky Cashin. **832** Meath. **833** Armagh. **834** John Owens. **835** Connacht hurlers. **836** Clare. **837** Boston. **838** Meath. **839** Clare. **840** Liam Turley.

CONNACHT GENERAL KNOWLEDGE – page 5

841 Mayo. **842** New York and Roscommon. **843** Corofin. **844** Joe McDonagh. **845** Michael Conneely. **846** Sligo. **847** Mattie Murphy. **848** Curry. **849** Two (Mayo and Roscommon). **850** Dessie Dolan (Senior). **851** Galway (2002 and 2003). **852** Four Roads. **853** FBD. **854** Nine (excluding replays in 1996 and 2004). **855** Annaghdown. **856** Tooreen. **857** St Mary's. **858** 1999. **859** Karol Mannion. **860** Galway (1986).

ACE OF CLUBS – page 87

861 Thirteen. **862** Six. **863** St Finbarr's (Cork). **864** St Finbarr's (Cork), UCD (Dublin) and Crossmaglen Rangers (Armagh). **865** Blackrock, Glen Rovers and St Finbarr's. **866** Sarsfields (Galway), Athenry (Galway) and Birr (Offaly). **867** Clann na nGael. **868** Birr and Ballyhale Shamrocks. **869** James Stephens. **870** Thurles Sarsfields. **871** 11. **872** Mount Sion. **873** St Joseph's Doora-Barefield (Clare). **874** Toomevara. **875** Corofin (Galway). **876** Laune Rangers. **877** Walsh Island. **878** Errigal Ciaran. **879** Burren (Down). **880** Four.

GAA PLAYERS WHO MADE A BIG IMPACT IN THEIR FIRST FULL SEASON – page 89

881 Two. **882** Three. **883** Maurice Fitzgerald. **884** Jason Sherlock. **885** Setanta O hAilpin. **886** Ronan Clarke. **887** One. **888** 2001. **889** 2002. **890** Richie Murray. **891** Ollie Baker. **892** Brian Corcoran. **893** Tommy Walsh. **894** Stephen Byrne (Offaly). **895** Stephen O'Neill. **896** 2002. **897** Mike Frank Russell. **898** 1998. **899** Eugene O'Neill. **900** Kevin O'Neill.

TRAINERS – page 91

901 Armagh. **902** Pat Flanagan. **903** Jerry Wallis. **904** Tyrone (2003). **905** Kilkenny. **906** Derry, Fermanagh, Cavan and Monaghan. **907** Galway (2005). **908** Clare (2002). **909** Michael Dempsey. **910** Limerick. **911** John Morrison. **912** Waterford. **913** Tipperary. **914** Tipperary (2001). **915** John Morrison. **916** Teddy Owens. **917** Mike McNamara. **918** Fiona O'Driscoll. **919** Fergal McCann. **920** Dave Moriarty (Limerick).

THE TOP 20 SCORERS IN ALL-IRELAND HURLING FINALS (PRIOR TO 2007) – page 93

921 Eddie Keher. **922** Jimmy Doyle. **923** Christy Ring. **924** Seven.

925 Nine. **926** Six. **927** Four. **928** Limerick. **929** Donie Nealon.
930 Kilkenny. **931** Six. **932** Kilkenny. **933** Nicky English. **934** 1985 and
1986. **935** 1983. **936** Wexford. **937** Three. **938** Seven. **939** 1967.
940 Kevin Hennessy.

MUNSTER GENERAL KNOWLEDGE – page 95
941 Pat Tobin. **942** Ollie Moran. **943** James Masters. **944** Ballygunner.
945 Finuge. **946** Mickey Ned O'Sullivan. **947** St Senan's, Kilkee.
948 Sixmilebridge (two), St Joseph's Doora-Barefield (two), Wolfe Tones
Shannon, Clarecastle. **949** Stevie Brenner. **950** Cork in 2000. **951** Gerry
Kennedy. **952** Derek Kavanagh. **953** 2003. **954** 2001. **955** 2004.
956 Patrickswell (2003). **957** Cork (2005). **958** Timmy McCarthy (2002 v
Galway). **959** Dan Shanahan (2), John Mullane, Eoin Kelly and Paul
Flynn. **960** Con Roche, Jimmy Barry Murphy, Donal O'Grady, John Allen,
Gerald McCarthy (All Cork) and John Meyler (Wexford).

CLUBCALL 2 – page 97
961 Cork. **962** Waterford. **963** Kerry. **964** Clare. **965** Down.
966 Tipperary. **967** Limerick. **968** Cavan. **969** Galway. **970** Leitrim.
971 Roscommon. **972** Dublin. **973** Down. **974** Westmeath. **975** Wexford.
976 Tyrone. **977** Sligo. **978** Laois. **979** Fermanagh. **980** Louth.

GENERAL KNOWLEDGE – page 98
981 2000. **982** Richie Connor. **983** James Stephens. **984** Ballinasloe
(Galway). **985** Kilmacud Crokes. **986** James Flemming. **987** Waterford IT.
988 Paul Bealin. **989** Jim McKernan. **990** Cork (2005 and 2006). **991** Len
Gaynor. **992** Derry City. **993** Jimmy McGuinness. **994** Scotstown.
995 Oisin McConville (2004 and 2005). **996** Dungiven (Derry) – St
Canice's are the football club and Kevin Lynch's are the hurling club.
997 Adrian Cush. **998** 1968. **999** Joe Dooley. **1000** Martin Furlong.

MANAGERIAL ROLL CALL 2 – page 100
1001 Fergal O'Donnell. **1002** Luke Dempsey. **1003** Four. **1004** Pat Holmes
and Noel Connelly. **1005** Martin Fogarty. **1006** Liam Sheedy. **1007** Down
minors. **1008** John Hardiman. **1009** Ballyhale Shamrocks (All-Ireland
club hurling title). **1010** One. **1011** Tony Leahy. **1012** Salthill/
Knocknacarra (All-Ireland club football title). **1013** Abbey CBS Newry

(All-Ireland colleges football title). **1014** Portumna (All-Ireland club hurling). **1015** Eoin Garvey. **1016** Seamus Qualter. **1017** Sos Dowling. **1018** London to the Nicky Rackard title. **1019** John Mitchell. **1020** Pat O'Connor.

GAA AUTOBIOGRAPHIES – page 102

1021 Liam Hayes. **1022** Ger Loughnane. **1023** Dessie Farrell. **1024** Davy Fitzgerald. **1025** Mickey Harte. **1026** Charlie Carter. **1027** Pat Spillane. **1028** Liam Dunne. **1029** Dermot Earley. **1030** Terence McNaughton. **1031** John O'Leary. **1032** Colm O'Rourke. **1033** Justin McCarthy. **1034** Graham Geraghty. **1035** Brian Corcoran. **1036** Cyril Farrell. **1037** Mike McNamara. **1038** Nicky English. **1039** Jack O'Connor. **1040** Oisin McConville.

HURLING GENERAL KNOWLEDGE – page 103

1041 Peter Barry. **1042** Pat Cronin. **1043** Tony Griffin. **1044** Larry O'Gorman. **1045** Kieran Murphy (Sarsfields). **1046** Martin Hanamy. **1047** De La Salle. **1048** 1996. **1049** Martin Storey. **1050** 1999. **1051** Louth. **1052** 1992. **1053** Killeagh. **1054** Johnny Pilkington. **1055** Tom Ryan. **1056** Donal Og Cusack. **1057** 2002 and 2003. **1058** Mike McNamara. **1059** Galway and Dublin. **1060** Eamonn Cregan.

LEINSTER HURLING FINALS – page 105

1061 John O'Connor. **1062** 11. **1063** Seven. **1064** Six. **1065** Henry Shefflin. **1066** 2002. **1067** 1991. **1068** Paul Codd. **1069** Billy Byrne. **1070** 1985. **1071** David Hughes. **1072** One (1999). **1073** 1961. **1074** 1949. **1075** 1993. **1076** Liam Coughlan. **1077** Nine. **1078** 1993. **1079** 1998. **1080** Michael Kavanagh.

FOOTBALLERS AND THEIR CLUBS 1 – page 107

1081 Killeavy. **1082** Enniskillen Gaels. **1083** Kilmacud Crokes. **1084** Caltra. **1085** Killanerin. **1086** Mayobridge. **1087** St Gall's. **1088** Crossmolina Deel Rovers. **1089** Croom. **1090** Arles/Kilcruise. **1091** Clann na nGael. **1092** Rhode. **1093** Clonguish. **1094** Gaoth Dobhair. **1095** Trim. **1096** Bantry Blues. **1097** Glenullin. **1098** Moyle Rovers. **1099** Allenwood. **1100** Garrycastle.

COUNTY SWITCHERS – page 108

1101 Cavan. **1102** Waterford. **1103** Cork. **1104** Dublin. **1105** Waterford. **1106** Cork. **1107** Kildare. **1108** Tipperary. **1109** Kildare before returning to Tipperary. **1110** Laois. **1111** Mayo. **1112** Down. **1113** Derry. **1114** Kildare before returning to Carlow. **1115** Cork. **1116** Offaly. **1117** Tipperary before returning to Limerick. **1118** Dublin. **1119** Wicklow. **1120** Limerick.

GENERAL KNOWLEDGE – page 109

1121 Down (1987). **1122** Sean Og de Paor. **1123** Davy Fitzgerald, Anthony Daly, Brian Lohan, Sean McMahon, Ollie Baker and Jamesie O'Connor. **1124** Paddy Moriarty (1972). **1125** Tomas Mulcahy (hurling), Larry Tompkins (football). **1126** Tadhgie Murphy. **1127** Pairc Ui Chaoimh. **1128** John Hudson. **1129** Luke Dempsey. **1130** Noel Skehan. **1131** Denis Taylor. **1132** Larry Stanley. **1133** Gerry McEntee (Meath) in 1988, Colm O'Neill (Cork) in 1990, Tony Davis (Cork) in 1993, Charlie Redmond (Dublin) in 1995, Liam McHale (Mayo) in 1996 and Colm Coyle (Meath) in 1996. **1134** John Keane. **1135** John Joe O'Reilly. **1136** Mick Mackey. **1137** Sean O'Neill. **1138** Brian Lohan (Clare). **1139** St Finbarr's. **1140** Four (not including 1995 replay).

COUNTY NICKNAMES – page 111

1141 Cork. **1142** Antrim. **1143** Cavan. **1144** Derry. **1145** Kildare. **1146** Down. **1147** Meath. **1148** Tipperary. **1149** Laois. **1150** Offaly. **1151** Wexford. **1152** Monaghan. **1153** Sligo. **1154** Westmeath. **1155** Armagh. **1156** Wicklow. **1157** Limerick. **1158** Donegal. **1159** Tyrone. **1160** Carlow.

GENERAL KNOWLEDGE – page 112

1161 Alan Keane. **1162** 1939. **1163** 1985. **1164** Peter McDermott. **1165** Paddy O'Rourke. **1166** Ballyhegan. **1167** Pat McEnaney and Brian White. **1168** Dickie Murphy. **1169** Seamus Moynihan, Darragh O Se, Mike Frank Russell. **1170** Sixmilebridge. **1171** Dinny Allen. **1172** Three. **1173** Omagh CBS. **1174** Carrickmore. **1175** Graham Geraghty, Trevor Giles, Conor Martin and Enda McManus. **1176** Cushendall. **1177** 1998 All-Ireland semi-final between Offaly and Clare. **1178** Donal Og Cusack. **1179** Ross and Aidan Carr (Down). **1180** Ger Fitzgerald (1992), Mark Landers (1999), Pat Mulcahy (2006).

HURLING ALL-STARS – page 114
1181 2003. **1182** Jamesie O'Connor and Brian Lohan. **1183** DJ Carey
(nine). **1184** Seven. **1185** Brian McMahon. **1186** Seamus Durack (Clare).
1187 Ben and Jerry O'Connor (Cork). **1188** Ger McGrattan (1992).
1189 John Connolly. **1190** Nicky English. **1191** Pat Critchley (1985).
1192 Tony O'Sullivan. **1193** Brian Whelehan (1994). **1194** David
Kilcoyne (1986). **1195** 1992. **1196** Brian and Frank Lohan (Clare),
Andy and Martin Comerford (Kilkenny), Paul and Eoin Kelly (Tipperary),
Joe and Johnny Dooley (Offaly), Sean Og and Setanta O hAilpin (Cork),
Ben and Jerry O'Connor (Cork). **1197** Three. **1198** Joe McKenna.
1199 Jimmy and Joe Cooney. **1200** Pat, Ger and John Henderson
(Kilkenny), Cormac, Colm and Conal Bonnar (Tipperary), Joe, Johnny
and Billy Dooley (Offaly).

ULSTER FOOTBALL FINALS – page 116
1201 2005. **1202** 2001. **1203** Six. **1204** Four (excluding the replays).
1205 Oisin McConville. **1206** Dan Gordon. **1207** Derry. **1208** Down.
1209 Joe Brolly. **1210** He became the highest scoring player in Ulster
championship history. **1211** Paul McGrane. **1212** Sean Teague. **1213** Four.
1214 Cavan. **1215** Seamus McEnaney. **1216** Four. **1217** Stephen King.
1218 Paddy McKeever. **1219** 1970. **1220** Johnny McBride.

CONTROVERSIES – page 118
1221 Jimmy Cooney. **1222** Derry. **1223** 'The Ban'. **1224** Rule 21.
1225 Brian Mullins, Ray Hazley, Ciaran Duff (Dublin) and Tomas Tierney
(Galway). **1226** Carlow. **1227** Tony Keady. **1228** Tony Davis. **1229** Colin
Lynch. **1230** Colm Coyle (Meath) and Liam McHale (Mayo). **1231** The
'Three stripes affair'. **1232** 2002. **1233** John Gough. **1234** Cork.
1235 Bendix. **1236** Paddy Power. **1237** John McEntee. **1238** Sean Og O
hAilpin, Donal Og Cusack, Diarmuid O'Sullivan (Cork), Andrew Quinn,
Alan Markham, Barry Nugent, Colin Lynch (Clare). **1239** The RDS affair.
1240 1911.

**FOOTBALLERS WHO HAVE PLAYED IN ALL-IRELAND FINALS OVER
THE LAST 15 YEARS** – page 121
1241 Cork. **1242** Meath. **1243** Kerry. **1244** Mayo. **1245** Mayo. **1246** Derry.
1247 Dublin. **1248** Meath. **1249** Down. **1250** Mayo. **1251** Armagh.

1252 Tyrone. **1253** Kerry. **1254** Mayo. **1255** Donegal. **1256** Meath.
1257 Kerry. **1258** Kerry. **1259** Galway. **1260** Mayo.

FAMOUS GAA FAMILIES – page 122

1261 John, Joe and Michael Connolly. **1262** Pat, Mick and Tom Spillane.
1263 Mick and Karl O'Dwyer. **1264** Nicky, Bobby and Billy Rackard.
1265 James McCartan and James McCartan. **1266** Gus Lohan.
1267 Kevin, Sean, Ger and Liam Fennelly. **1268** The Cooneys. **1269** Tom
and Jim Cashman. **1270** Richie and Phil Bennis. **1271** Johnny and Declan
Pilkington, Jim and John Troy, Joe, Billy and Johnny Dooley. **1272** Matt
and Richie (brothers), and Tomas and Liam (brothers). **1273** Sean Og,
Setanta and Aisake O hAilpin. **1274** The McManuses. **1275** Kerry. **1276**
The Kernan family and the Harte family. **1277** Pat Henderson. **1278**
Paddy, Phil 'Fan' and Philly Larkin. **1279** Dan, Martin, Pat and John
Quigley. **1280** Mick O'Dwyer (Kildare) and John O'Dwyer (Kerry).

GENERAL KNOWLEDGE – page 124

1281 Donegal. **1282** Philip Brennan. **1283** Damien McClearn.
1284 Newtownshandrum (Cork). **1285** 2005. **1286** 2000. **1287** Donegal
and Mayo. **1288** Armagh. **1289** Six. **1290** 1989. **1291** Moorefield.
1292 Brendan Lynskey. **1293** Tommy Breheny. **1294** London.
1295 Wicklow. **1296** 2006. **1297** 2001. **1298** Cavan. **1299** Declan Ryan
(Tipperary). **1300** Sean Lowry.

LEINSTER FOOTBALL FINALS – page 126

1301 Three. **1302** Two. **1303** Tommy Lyons. **1304** Tomas Quinn.
1305 Meath. **1306** Seven. **1307** David O'Shaughnessy. **1308** Paddy
Christie. **1309** Meath. **1310** 2005. **1311** Four (excluding the 2004 replay).
1312 1995. **1313** Ross Munnelly. **1314** Four. **1315** Ollie Murphy. **1316** Brian
Murphy. **1317** Finbarr Cullen. **1318** Alan Mangan. **1319** Dermot Earley and
Tadhg Fennin. **1320** Tadhg Fennin.

HURLING GOALS GALORE – page 128

1321 Aidan Fogarty. **1322** Ben O'Connor. **1323** Michael Jacob.
1324 Eugene O'Neill and Liam Cahill. **1325** David Forde. **1326** DJ Carey
and Henry Shefflin. **1327** Tommy Quaid. **1328** Charlie Carter. **1329** Tom
Dempsey. **1330** Alan Kerins. **1331** Eoin Kelly. **1332** Niall Healy.

1333 Michael Cleary (although it took a deflection off Liam Walsh's hurley). **1334** Ger Manley. **1335** PJ Delaney. **1336** Dan Shanahan. **1337** Martin Comerford. **1338** Johnny Pilkington. **1339** Noel Lane (Galway). **1340** Tommy Coen.

MATCH THE HURLER TO HIS COUNTY – page 130
1341 Clare. **1342** Cork. **1343** Kilkenny. **1344** Laois. **1345** Waterford. **1346** Offaly. **1347** Dublin. **1348** Down. **1349** Carlow. **1350** Westmeath. **1351** Tipperary. **1352** Offaly. **1353** Limerick. **1354** Armagh. **1355** Kerry. **1356** Kildare. **1357** Offaly. **1358** Derry. **1359** London. **1360** Galway.

FOOTBALL GOALS GALORE – page 131
1361 Dara O Cinneide and Tomas O Se. **1362** Oisin McConville. **1363** Declan Meehan. **1364** Kevin O'Neill. **1365** Darren O'Sullivan. **1366** Jason Sherlock. **1367** Ciaran McManus. **1368** Mattie Forde. **1369** Mike Frank Russell. **1370** Barney Rock. **1371** Owen Mulligan. **1372** Alan Dillon. **1373** Andrew McCann. **1374** James McCartan. **1375** Louth. **1376** Eoin Brosnan. **1377** Benny Coulter. **1378** Peter Canavan. **1379** Ollie Murphy. **1380** Billy O'Sullivan.

GREAT COMEBACKS – page 133
1381 Johnny Dooley and Pat O'Connor. **1382** Aidan Ryan. **1383**. Andy Moran. **1384** Wexford. **1385** Laois. **1386** Colm Coyle. **1387** Galway. **1388** Castlehaven. **1389** Erins Own (Cork). **1390** Kevin Foley. **1391** David Beggy. **1392** Tony O'Sullivan and Seanie O'Leary. **1393** Kevin Hennessy, Tomas Mulcahy, John Fitzgibbon (2) and Mark Foley. **1394** Kilkenny. **1395** Derry. **1396** Frankie Carroll. **1397** Christy Ring. **1398** Wexford. **1399** Ray Sampson. **1400** Meath.

MATCH THE FOOTBALLER TO HIS COUNTY – page 136
1401 Longford. **1402** Louth. **1403** Clare. **1404** Limerick. **1405** Westmeath. **1406** Offaly. **1407** Cork. **1408** Sligo. **1409** Antrim. **1410** Kildare. **1411** Cavan. **1412** Derry. **1413** Roscommon. **1414** Wexford. **1415** Monaghan. **1416** Fermanagh. **1417** Leitrim. **1418** Offaly. **1419** Armagh. **1420** Down.

FOOTBALL PENALTIES SCORED AND MISSED – page 137
1421 Trevor Giles. **1422** Ronan Sweeney. **1423** Ciaran McDonald.
1424 Paul Bealin. **1425** Declan O'Keeffe. **1426** Martin Furlong.
1427 Mayo. **1428** Dara O Cinneide. **1429** Kevin O'Dwyer. **1430** Maurice
Sheridan. **1431** John Cleary. **1432** Paddy Cullen. **1433** Kevin McCabe.
1434 Charlie Redmond. **1435** Brian Stafford. **1436** Keith Barr. **1437** Glen
Ryan. **1438** Charlie Redmond. **1439** Neil Collins. **1440** Bill McCorry.

CONTROVERSIAL SCORES THAT WERE AND WEREN'T REGISTERED
– page 140
1441 Johnny Flaherty. **1442** Longford. **1443** Tommy Doyle. **1444** Gerry
Murphy. **1445** Declan Ryan. **1446** Brian Morley. **1447** Brendan Devenny.
1448 Sean McLaughlin. **1449** Richie Bennis. **1450** Jim Troy. **1451** Padraig
Horan. **1452** Damien Martin. **1453** Cavan in the 1997 Ulster final.
1454 Alan Brogan. **1455** John Moloney. **1456** Nicky English. **1457** Cork.
1458 Ted Morrissey. **1459** Jimmy Murray. **1460** Shane Curran.

CLUB CALL 3 – page 144
1461 Antrim. **1462** Clare. **1463** Cork. **1464** Louth. **1465** Galway.
1466 Tyrone. **1467** Monaghan. **1468** Donegal. **1469** Waterford.
1470 Kilkenny. **1471** Wexford. **1472** Offaly. **1473** Mayo. **1474** Meath.
1475 Limerick. **1476** Dublin. **1477** Tipperary. **1478** Kerry. **1479** Derry.
1480 Kerry.

NAME THE YEAR 2 – page 145
1481 1986. **1482** 2000. **1483** 2000. **1484** 1996. **1485** 1998. **1486** 2003.
1487 1988. **1488** 1991. **1489** 1978. **1490** 1985. **1491** 1997. **1492** 1989.
1493 2001. **1494** 1996. **1495** 1996. **1496** 2001. **1497** 2001. **1498** 2004.
1499 2002. **1500** 2006.

MINOR MATTERS - THE LAST 15 YEARS – page 147
1501 1996. **1502** 2006. **1503** 1992. **1504** 2003. **1505** 1998. **1506** Laois
(2003). **1507** 1995. **1508** Down (2005). **1509** Three. **1510** 1999. **1511** 1998.
1512 2001. **1513** 2003. **1514** None. **1515** 1997. **1516** Two (1994 and 1995).
1517 1996. **1518** 1993. **1519** Cork. **1520** Charlie (senior) and Cathal
McCarthy.

HURLING SCORES FROM PLACED BALLS – page 149
1521 Jamesie O'Connor. **1522** John Fenton. **1523** Paul Flynn. **1524** DJ Carey. **1525** Ollie Baker. **1526** Johnny Dooley. **1527** David Fitzgerald. **1528** Ben O'Connor. **1529** Henry Shefflin. **1530** Damien Fitzhenry. **1531** Sean McMahon. **1532** Andrew O'Shaughnessy. **1533** Andy Comerford. **1534** Jamesie O'Connor. **1535** Stephen Power. **1536** Cathal Casey. **1537** Damien Fitzhenry. **1538** Pat Fox. **1539** Niall Gilligan. **1540** Martin Storey.

UNDER-21 QUESTIONS FROM THE LAST 15 YEARS – page 152
1541 1995. **1542** Two. **1543** 1995 and 1996 (the 1995 football final was a draw and the replay was played in Thurles). **1544** One. **1545** 2000. **1546** Four. **1547** 1995. **1548** 2004. **1549** Aidan Canning. **1550** 1993. **1551** 2002. **1552** Michael Fennelly. **1553** Five. **1554** 2003. **1555** Eugene Cloonan. **1556** 1996. **1557** 1994. **1558** Three. **1559** 1996. **1560** Barry Cullinane (with Galway in 2005).

FOOTBALLERS AND THEIR CLUBS 2 – page 154
1561 Corofin. **1562** Na Fianna. **1563** St Eunan's, Letterkenny. **1564** Killeavy (Armagh). **1565** Rathmore. **1566** Moy. **1567** Crossmolina Deel Rovers. **1568** Salthill/Knocknacarra. **1569** Dromore. **1570** Pearse Og. **1571** Mountbellew-Moylough. **1572** Clan na Gael. **1573** Ballyboden St Enda's. **1574** Ballinderry. **1575** Naomh Aban. **1576** St Michael's. **1577** Moorefield. **1578** Tubber. **1579** Timahoe. **1580** Rathmore.

NAME THE MISSING LINK IN THE LINE OR THE PARTNERSHIP – page 155
1581 Colm O'Rourke. **1582** Gerry McInerney. **1583** Sean McMahon. **1584** Padraig Joyce. **1585** Colm Cooper. **1586** Mikey Sheehy. **1587** Darren Fay. **1588** Anthony Tohill. **1589** Noel Tierney. **1590** Sean Doherty. **1591** Gerry McEntee. **1592** Conor Hayes. **1593** Kevin Martin. **1594** Liam Dunne. **1595** Sean Og O hAilpin. **1596** Ray Cummins. **1597** Nicky English. **1598** Frank Lohan. **1599** Johnny Crowley. **1600** John Doyle.

CRUCIAL AND OUTSTANDING FOOTBALL SCORES FROM PLACED BALLS – page 156
1601 Maurice Fitzgerald. **1602** Dessie Dolan. **1603** Peter Canavan.

1604 Ja Fallon. **1605** Cian Ward. **1606** Tomas Quinn. **1607** Peter Canavan. **1608** Niall Finnegan. **1609** Ger Cavlan. **1610** Ciaran McManus. **1611** Larry Tompkins. **1612** Peter Canavan. **1613** Colm Bradley. **1614** Pascal Kelleghan. **1615** Seamus Aldridge. **1616** Shane Curran (Roscommon v Sligo – Connacht semi-final replay). **1617** Maurice Fitzgerald. **1618** Brian Stafford. **1619** Larry Tompkins. **1620** Eamonn McEneaney.

GENERAL KNOWLEDGE – page 159
1621 1964, 1965 and 1966. **1622** Gary Ruane. **1623** 1998 (he played his last game against Clare that summer). **1624** 1997. **1625** Billy Morgan. **1626** Peter Ford. **1627** Tommy Breheny (Sligo). **1628** Na Fianna (Dublin). **1629** Duffry Rovers. **1630** Padraig Joyce. **1631** Anthony Finnerty. **1632** Charlie Redmond. **1633** Louth. **1634** Liam Hodgins. **1635** Alan Kerins (with Clarinbridge and Salthill/Knocknacarra). **1636** Ciaran, Brendan and Michael Herron. **1637** Joey McLoughney. **1638** Brian Carroll (son of late Pat Carroll). **1639** Tony Hanahoe (Dublin – 1976-79). **1640** Charlie Redmond and Trevor Giles.

LEGENDS OF HURLING AND FOOTBALL – page 161
1641 Walsh Island. **1642** 18. **1643** Rathnure. **1644** Four. **1645** One. **1646** Tullaroan. **1647** Three. **1648** 1969. **1649** Tuam Stars. **1650** Four. **1651** Four. **1652** Glenflesk. **1653** St Mary's Cahirciveen and Leixlip. **1654** Six. **1655** Two. **1656** Holycross-Ballycahill. **1657** Two. **1658** Newry Mitchell's. **1659** 1979. **1660** Two.

MUNSTER'S FINEST HURLERS – WHO AM I? – page 163
1661 Mick Roche. **1662** Tony O'Sullivan. **1663** Pat Hartigan. **1664** Eamonn Cregan. **1665** Jackie Power. **1666** Sean Stack. **1667** Joe McKenna. **1668** Gerald McCarthy. **1669** John Fenton. **1670** Ciaran Carey. **1671** Brian Lohan. **1672** Pat Fox. **1673** Gary Kirby. **1674** Sean McMahon. **1675** Donie Nealon. **1676** Phil Grimes. **1677** Charlie McCarthy. **1678** John Leahy. **1679** Seanie O'Leary. **1680** Tom Cheasty.

ODD ONE OUT – page 166
1681 James McGarry (McGarry is a hurling goalkeeper while the other two are football goalkeepers). **1682** Lavey (Lavey is in Derry while the

other two are in Down). **1683** Ronan Curran (Curran is from St Finbarr's while the other two play with Cloyne). **1684** Irish Press Cup (Irish Press Cup is for All-Ireland minor hurling championships while the other two are for All-Ireland club championships). **1685** Toomevara (Toomevara have never won an All-Ireland club hurling title while the other two have). **1686** Castlehaven (Castlehaven never won an All-Ireland club football title while the other two have). **1687** Jack Boothman (Boothman was a GAA President from Wicklow while the other two were President's from Kilkenny). **1688** Darragh O Se (O Se never captained Kerry to an All-Ireland senior title while the other two did). **1689** Kilmessan (Kilmessan is in Meath while the other two are in Laois). **1690** Tony Davis (Davis didn't captain Cork to an All-Ireland senior football title while the other two did). **1691** Nally Stand (Nally Stand is no longer part of Croke Park while the other two are). **1692** Martin Comerford (Martin Comerford didn't captain Kilkenny to an All-Ireland senior hurling title while the other two did). **1693** Pearse Stadium (Pearse Stadium is in Connacht while the other two are in Munster). **1694** Portaferry (Portaferry is in Down while the other two are in Antrim). **1695** De La Salle (De La Salle have never won a Munster club hurling title while the other two have). **1696** Na Fianna (Na Fianna never won an All-Ireland club football title while the other two have). **1697** Mike Houlihan (Houlihan was from Kilmallock while the other two played with Patrickswell. Kirby and Carey also captained Limerick to Munster senior hurling titles).

1698 Knockmore (Knockmore have never won an All-Ireland club football title while the other two have). **1699** Athenry (Athenry have won three All-Ireland club hurling titles while the other two have won four).
1700 Stuart Reynolds (Reynolds is a football goalkeeper while the other two are hurling goalkeepers).

GENERAL KNOWLEDGE – page 167
1701 Archbishop Croke. **1702** NFL Final 1991 – Dublin v Kildare. **1703** Matthew Clancy. **1704** 130 metres and 80 metres. **1705** Dan Shanahan. **1706** Martin Clarke. **1707** Laois. **1708** 65. **1709** Alan and Bernard Brogan. **1710** It was the first time that two colleges reached the final despite not having won their provincial championships. **1711** The Inky Flaherty Cup. **1712** Kilkenny CBS. **1713** David Kennedy and Paddy O'Brien (both played with Tipperary in 2001 and Kildare in 2007). **1714** Downpatrick.

1715 Andrew Smyth. **1716** Cyril Farrell, Joe McDonagh, Joe Connolly and Pat Fleury. **1717** New York. **1718** St Jarlath's Park. **1719** Rounders. **1720** Sean McMahon (Clare).

MUNSTER FOOTBALL FINALS – page 170

1721 2002. **1722** Paddy O'Shea. **1723** 2000. **1724** Cork. **1725** Seven. **1726** 1991. **1727** Three. **1728** Liam Kearns. **1729** Francis McInerney. **1730** John Quane. **1731** Mike McCarthy. **1732** Declan O'Sullivan. **1733** 1986. **1734** Colm Cooper. **1735** One (1898). **1736** Fifteen. **1737** 1992. **1738** Donncha O'Connor. **1739** Eoin Keating. **1740** Colm Clancy and Martin Daly.

HURLING GOALKEEPERS – page 172

1741 Fenians, Johnstown. **1742** Three. **1743** Michael Crimmins. **1744** Joe Dermody. **1745** Ballybacon-Grange. **1746** Three. **1747** Stephen Byrne. **1748** Ballygalget. **1749** Kerry. **1750** Ballyboden-St Enda's. **1751** Donal Og Cusack. **1752** Terence Murray. **1753** Ian O'Regan. **1754** Antrim. **1755** Peter Murphy. **1756** Noel Skehan (1982) and Ger Cunningham (1986). **1757** David 'Stoney' Burke. **1758** Anthony Nash. **1759** John Commins (Galway – 1986). **1760** James McGarry.

NATIONAL FOOTBALL LEAGUE FINALS – page 174

1761 Three. **1762** Kieran McGeeney. **1763** 2000. **1764** Mayo. **1765** Offaly. **1766** Eamonn McGee, Rory Kavanagh, Adrian Sweeney. **1767** Kevin O'Neill. **1768** Four. **1769** Peter Canavan. **1770** 2002. **1771** Steven McDonnell. **1772** 1993. **1773** 1997. **1774** 1999. **1775** Anthony Tohill. **1776** 1998. **1777** 2004. **1778** 1996. **1779** 1985. **1780** Mayo.

FOOTBALL GOALKEEPERS – page 176

1781 John Devine. **1782** Declan O'Keeffe (2002). **1783** Donal Smyth. **1784** Martin McNamara. **1785** Paul O'Dowd. **1786** Ken O'Halloran. **1787** Paddy Linden. **1788** Longford. **1789** James Hanrahan. **1790** Paul Hearty. **1791** Institute of Technology Sligo. **1792** John Cooper (Wexford). **1793** John O'Leary. **1794** Billy Morgan (1973) and Martin Furlong (1982). **1795** Paddy Cullen. **1796** Aidan Skelton. **1797** Mick Pender. **1798** David Mitchell. **1799** Padraig Lally. **1800** Owensie Hoare (Roscommon – half-back in 1943, goalkeeper in 1944) and Johnny

Culloty (Kerry, corner-forward in 1955 and goalkeeper in 1959, 1962, 1969 and 1970).

FOOTBALL ALL-STARS – page 178
1801 Pat Spillane (nine). **1802** Martin and James McHugh. **1803** Fergal Byron. **1804** John Keane and Dessie Dolan. **1805** Matt and Richie Connor, Tomas and Liam Connor, Brendan and Sean Lowry. **1806** Francie Grehan (2001). **1807** 1994. **1808** Paul Galvin (Kerry – 2004). **1809** Kenneth and Conor Mortimer. **1810** Martin O'Connell and Tommy Dowd. **1811** 1999. **1812** Barry Owens and Marty McGrath. **1813** Peter Canavan. **1814** Kildare. **1815** Derry. **1816** Paddy Reynolds. **1817** Anthony Tohill and Tony Scullion. **1818** Ger Power. **1819** Liam O'Neill (Galway - 1973), Kevin O'Neill (Mayo - 1993). **1820** Derry (1993).

ALL-IRELAND HURLING SEMI-FINALS OVER THE LAST 15 YEARS
– page 180
1821 Ten. **1822** Eoin Kelly. **1823** Seven. **1824** Jerry O'Connor. **1825** Eugene Cloonan. **1826** Galway. **1827** Johnny Dooley. **1828** 1995. **1829** Tipperary. **1830** 2002 (Clare v Waterford). **1831** 2003 (Cork v Wexford). **1832** 2005 (Cork v Clare). **1833** 1996. **1834** Six. **1835** Jimmy Coogan. **1836** Three. **1837** Michael Doyle. **1838** Paul Flynn. **1839** Niall Maloney. **1840** Morgan Darcy.

GENERAL KNOWLEDGE – page 182
1841 Two. **1842** John Kearns. **1843** Ger Cunningham. **1844** Four. **1845** 1984. **1846** Pete McGrath. **1847** Armagh and Antrim. **1848** Brian McEniff. **1849** Ten. **1850** Sean Flanagan and Tom Langan. **1851** Kerry v Offaly in 1980. **1852** Colm O'Rourke. **1853** Eight. **1854** Kevin McGourty. **1855** Kevin Heffernan. **1856** Tooreen. **1857** Ballina Stephenites. **1858** Burt. **1859** Colin Byrne. **1860** David Hickey, John McCarthy and Bernard Brogan.

LEADING 20 GOALSCORERS IN SENIOR HURLING CHAMPIONSHIPS FROM 1930 TO 2006 – page 184
1861 Nicky Rackard. **1862** Tony Doran. **1863** Seanie O'Leary. **1864** Eddie Keher. **1865** DJ Carey. **1866** Christy Ring. **1867** Limerick. **1868** Laois. **1869** Mick Mackey. **1870** Charlie McCarthy. **1871** Eamonn Cregan.

1872 Paddy Molloy. **1873** Jimmy Barry Murphy. **1874** Three. **1875** Cork. **1876** Three. **1877** Liam Fennelly. **1878** Paul Flynn. **1879** Kevin Hennessy. **1880** Nicky English.

CLASSIC FOOTBALL AND HURLING MATCHES OVER THE LAST 15 YEARS – page 186

1881 Ciaran McDonald. **1882** Eight. **1883** Steven McDonnell. **1884** Eamonn Cregan. **1885** Donegal. **1886** 1995 Leinster final between Offaly and Kilkenny. **1887** Steven McDonnell. **1888** Nine. **1889** Mickey Moran. **1890** Cork and Offaly. **1891** Joe Kavanagh. **1892** Jamesie O'Connor. **1893** Barry Duffy. **1894** Damien Howe. **1895** Seamus Downey. **1896** Joe Deane and Setanta O hAilpin. **1897** Val Daly. **1898** Eamonn Morrissey. **1899** Ciaran McCabe. **1900** Garvan McCarthy.

GENERAL KNOWLEDGE – page 188

1901 1992. **1902** Noel Skehan. **1903** Christy Ring and John Doyle. **1904** Sean O Siochain. **1905** Dan O Rourke and Dr Donal Keenan. **1906** Mikey Sheehy, Paidi O Se, Denis 'Ogie' Moran, Pat Spillane and Ger Power. **1907** Paidi O Se and Denis Ogie Moran. **1908** Brian Murphy. **1909** Ray Cummins. **1910** UCC. **1911** Cork. **1912** Ciaran Barr. **1913** Pat, Tom and Mick Spillane. **1914** Christy Walsh in 1992. **1915** Al Blue Lewis. **1916** 1988. **1917** Cork and Clare. **1918** Teddy McCarthy and Denis Walsh. **1919** Mossy and Brian Carroll. **1920** Stephen McNamara (1997) and Niall Gilligan (2007).

LEGENDARY SCORING FEATS AND SCORERS IN HURLING AND FOOTBALL – page 190

1921 Eddie Keher. **1922** Henry Shefflin. **1923** Matt Connor. **1924** Nicky English (2-12 v Antrim in 1989). **1925** Jimmy Keaveney (2-6 v Armagh in 1977). **1926** Mikey Sheehy (2-6 v Dublin in 1979). **1927** Nicky Rackard. **1928** Eugene Cloonan. **1929** Eddie Keher. **1930** Johnny Dooley. **1931** 2-10. **1932** Charlie McCarthy. **1933** Rory Gallagher (Fermanagh). **1934** Mikey Sheehy. **1935** Kildare. **1936** Mark Corrigan. **1937** Mick Mackey. **1938** Declan Darcy. **1939** Jimmy Smyth. **1940** Frank Stockwell.

GENERAL KNOWLEDGE – page 192

1941 Phil 'Fan' and Philip Larkin. **1942** Colin Lynch. **1943** (Kilkenny). **1944** Pat Hartigan (Limerick) and Eoin Kelly (Ti **1945** Eoin and Paul Kelly (Tipperary), Ollie and James Mor **1946** Paul McKillen (Antrim – 1993). **1947** Jack O'Shea. **194 Dowling. **1949** Des Foley. **1950** Peter Canavan and Liam H **1951** Johnny Enright. **1952** Mick Lyons. **1953** 1987 (Dundall Antrim). **1954** Johnny Dooley. **1955** Seven. **1956** Brian Lacey Tipperary). **1957** Larry Tompkins. **1958** Alan Kerins with Gal **1959** John Troy (Offaly). **1960** Sean Condon (Cork), Tony Wal Jimmy Doyle (Tipp) and Brian Cody (Kilkenny).

PROVINCIAL AND ALL-IRELAND CLUB HURLING – page

1961 1995. **1962** Loughgiel Shamrocks (1983). **1963** UCD. **196 **1965** Castlegar. **1966** Rathnure. **1967** O'Donovan Rossa's. **19 O'Loughlin Gaels. **1969** John McIntyre. **1970** Buffer's Alley. **1 Kiltormer and Cashel King Cormacs. **1972** Kilmallock. **1973 Sixmilebridge. **1974** 2002. **1975** O'Tooles. **1976** Clarecastle. Tremane and Four Roads. **1978** Sean Stack. **1979** Ballyhale and Kiltormer. **1980** John Horgan (Blackrock).

GENERAL KNOWLEDGE – page 196

1981 Ollie Moran. **1982** Laois in 1949. **1983** Jody Gormley. and Declan Carr. **1985** Diane O'Hora (Mayo ladies' football 1999). **1986** 1972. **1987** Alan Kerins. **1988** 1984 (although t to a replay and wasn't played for another month). **1989** Ty and Mayo in 2004 and 2006. **1990** Niall Healy. **1991** Damie (Galway) – he won Fitzgibbon with WIT and Sigerson with **1992** Kilkenny in 2003. **1993** Paddy Doherty. **1994** Peter C **1995** Rory McCarthy. **1996** Niall McNamee. **1997** John Doy and Jimmy Barry Murphy (Cork). **1998** Joe Considine (Clare **2000** Eddie Brennan (Kilkenny in 2000).